Priceless Heritage
The Future of Museums

by the same author

CELTIC ART
(*Faber*)

SCOTTISH GOLD AND SILVER WORK
(*Chatto and Windus*)

ART IN SCOTLAND
(*Oxford*)

SCOTTISH CRAFTS
(*Harrap*)

Priceless Heritage
The Future of Museums

IAN FINLAY

FABER AND FABER
3 Queen Square London WC1

*First published in 1977
by Faber and Faber Limited
3 Queen Square London WC1
Printed in Great Britain by
Latimer Trend & Company Ltd Plymouth*

ISBN 0 571 09107 5

© *Ian Finlay 1977*

For MARY

Contents

Preface

THIS BOOK is for the layman as much as for the professional. It is not an attempt to codify museum practices or policies. There are several manuals which do this admirably. It is written in the hope that it will set more people talking about the problems of museums as they talk about social and industrial problems, about politics and the professions and about other fields of activity of which they may or may not have any inside knowledge, but which their opinions may nevertheless in the long run help to influence. This, after all, is one of the ways in which democracy is supposed to work. But to the average person museums are a closed book, and as for talking about them he would not know where to begin.

Only a few out of many possible topics are brought together here, a few that seemed to me to be particularly significant. Naturally my thoughts owe much to colleagues I have had over forty years and more, but I shall not attempt to name any of them. I would, however, record my warm thanks to those who have read and commented on the MS of the book. First of them is the late Earl of Crawford and Balcarres, whose long and devoted championship of museums and galleries, and sage criticisms, have benefited so many who have worked in them. His death in 1975 was a sad loss. My publisher's specialist reader made many valuable suggestions, one of them the addition of the final chapter. Mr Giles de la Mare, as always, has been both encouraging and patient. Finally, I should like to include my gratitude to two people who, although they have not seen the book, made so many of its transatlantic references and comparisons possible many years ago, by initiating an invitation from the State Department for me to visit as many museums in the United States as I chose to select. They are the former Ambassador, Mr John Hay Whitney, and Mr Robert Clark, then of the American Embassy in London.

9

I Collections or Ideas

IN THE MINDS of most people, a museum is a collection, or a group of collections. We speak of the national collections when we mean the national museums and galleries, the state museums. The National Art-Collections Fund is there to help the museums and galleries of this country, large and small. 'Collection' and 'museum', in fact, come to be virtually interchangeable. So readily do we accept this identity of one with the other that I doubt if we have seriously questioned its validity in all the radical re-thinking about museums which is going on today.

Collecting is the expression of a deep-rooted human urge. One thinks of it as the obsession of individuals, but it is also a group urge. The community has not much apparent interest in buying masterpieces 'for the nation' or 'for the city', and often responds with expostulatory letters to the press; but anyone in a museum will tell you there is a never-ending trickle of modest gifts which arrive because the donor sees—or fancies he sees—some gap in the collections, and because he takes pride in helping those collections to expand. He does it not always because he wants to see his name on a label: many donors insist on anonymity. The 'friends of the museum' movement is a reflection of this pride. As with the occasional individual collector, the pride may be aggressive, vain, as when a prosperous citizenry sees in its museum a symbol of its success for all to note. However, on the whole it is an admirable sort of pride and has produced some memorable museum displays, particularly throughout the length and breadth of the United States. After all, it enables thousands of men and women of modest means to identify with something rather splendid, as they have tried to do in all ages—are the little figures in the limpid air of a Canaletto townscape not preening their pride in *duomo* and *campanile*? And if the public collection of today is linked with elaborate educational schemes and is seen to make a real contribution to the improvement of society, so much the better. But the

11

collection itself must grow. As a recent film about the National Gallery asserted in its final sequence, a collection which ceases to grow becomes fossilized; and not many people take pride in fossils.

There are of course static collections which are exceptions: collections once private, and now public. The Wallace Collection is an obvious example, and so is Apsley House. They are complete in themselves, documents of another age. In quite another way, so also is the Phillips Collection in Washington complete, in that it expresses the taste of one man, Duncan Phillips, and his wife. These have a special validity, either as footnotes to history or as the personal statements of men of discrimination and scholarship, which puts them in a category different from that of the normal museum.

This question of growth in a public collection poses many problems. Is growth really the only alternative to fossilization? There are certain limits to it. The excuse for growth is to render a collection more complete, more representative, but where does this lead? Such a purpose could end with megalomania. Representative collections may be attainable in natural history museums or science museums, where it is not so difficult to set certain bounds upon what is being represented. The arts, however, are too elusive to be caught in such convenient nets. Certainly, one may decide to present the main epochs in art history, but who is to say how many masters are needed to illustrate the various phases of an epoch, or how far one should go in trying to show the stages in development of this master or that? And to make it all more difficult, there is the patent impossibility of even beginning to fulfil such aims with a balanced display in an age when modest masters, let alone great ones, are in short supply in the art market. If expansion were the only alternative to fossilization, we should be faced with the ridiculous spectacle of curators of collections already magnificent watching the market in agonies of apprehension for ever trying to reconcile 'opportunities' with their very limited financial resources, aware that whatever they do their needs will never be satisfied. The private collector can stop when he likes, can sell or buy as he likes, can change the whole scope of his collection when he chooses and begin again. But if the museum is to be looked on as a collection one could argue that the curator must either bury his head comfortably in the sands of day-to-day minutiae of administration or raise his eyes to a prospect of insoluble problems.

The community's pride in adding to a public collection naturally enough is usually exceeded by the curator's. It is for the time being *his*, and he would not be human if he were not a little jealous for his charge. That is not to imply a foolish state of rivalry between the great institutions of the country for the ownership of outstanding works, for the truth is quite otherwise, and indeed it can, and does, happen that one museum, short of the necessary funds, will beg another to enter the bidding to save a coveted piece from going abroad. But when all is said and done, the importance-rating of museums remains far too closely associated with what they are able to acquire, and in them there still lingers on some of the status-symbol tradition which they inherited from the princes of the Renaissance, or indeed from industrial tycoons. Inflated prices and the panic rush to meet them have perhaps blinded us to where the situation is leading us. Not that I am trying to devalue our treasures, or to suggest we have so many we can afford to let some of them go. The artistic possessions of a country are a great part of its heritage, and where they are the products of its own artists or craftsmen I believe their export should be subject to yet stricter regulations than there are: not for any reason of prestige, but because they are part of us and their outgoing diminishes us. There is a difference between coveting something for a particular collection and saving for the nation something which is part of it.

The traditional emphasis on the collecting function of museums has produced in staff, probably at all levels, attitudes which it is difficult to change. There was always a tendency to recruit enthusiasts for collecting, and although a boyhood bent for beetles might be re-directed to Diptera, or postage stamps to prints, it was a simple translation from amateur to professional status, and commitment for life. Predictably, in many museums this has produced a curious, haphazard kind of progress. The collections would grow in an ungainly, leapfrog fashion, according to the predilections of successive collectors. The collection of French furniture might develop while the English remained static for ten or twenty years, simply because the reigning curator happened to be interested in and an authority on the former. No one has worried very much about this sort of progression, believing that it should work out all right in the end, yet it means there has been a sad tale of opportunities missed in certain neglected fields in museums which could not afford to have a large complement of specialists. To an outsider, it must seem too irrational to be true. Yet at one time such irrational 'policy' was normal, and we all know that in one great institution until not so many decades ago the trustees were so influenced by their classical upbringing and background that they were reputed to frown on the acquisition of antiquities other than Greek or Roman!

This sublime eccentricity could happen only when a public museum is looked upon as a private collection, not as a means of enlightenment for the public whose taxes pay for it. Most museums now will claim their acquisitions fit a predetermined plan, in so far as a plan is possible at all; but however good the intentions, in the art field at least tastes and chance ultimately play the biggest part in determining how a collection will expand. The domination of museums by the collecting tradition is reached with the coming of what might be called the tycoon type to the director's chair. This is perhaps primarily an American phenomenon. It involves the appointment of someone—it goes without saying, someone of excellent taste and long administrative experience—whose main job is to persuade people of wealth and good will to perpetuate their names by donating masterpieces or money, or both. Like most of those who have spent much of their lives in trying to acquire gifts for their museums, I am filled with envy at the powers of persuasion which such people display. But I hope I shall not be accused of sour grapes if I suggest that this sort of enticement does not seem to me to be the proper function of the head of a great museum in the second half of the twentieth century.

I well understand if a high proportion of existing curatorial staffs look with suspicion and even dismay upon criticism of the collecting concept of museums. For them, there is a certain *mystique* in a collection. They look on themselves as the inheritors of an inviolable corpus of material for the preservation of which they hold a stewardship, and they believe that though they may add to this corpus of material, neither they nor anyone may take away from it. I have deep respect for this point of view. It is found in museums of natural history and science just as frequently as in museums of art. Custodians of collections of Crustacea or

Lepidoptera may be just as sure of the sacredness of their charge as the custodian of a cabinet of Raphael cartoons. I would certainly not see such dedication interfered with. Anyone who in his researches has been frustrated by the irresponsibility of the 'caretaker' of some small museum who has allowed a vital link in a chain to disappear will bless the vigilant custodian. But sooner or later in every museum the problem has to be faced of how to accommodate accumulations of material for which there is no longer room, or whether to break the spell of ages and become ruthlessly selective. This problem particularly concerns the national museums, sacredest cows in the herd.

If museums are not collections, then what are they?

The notion of the museum with a mission is a century old, and more. In 1852 the Department of Practical Art was set up to establish, among other things, museums to study 'the common principles of taste', and five years later came the complex of institutions for investigating the arts and sciences known as the South Kensington Museum, which grew into the Victoria and Albert and Science Museums. It was an imaginative concept of the Prince Consort, reflected also in the Museum of Science and Art, now the Royal Scottish Museum, in Edinburgh. Already, in America, the collections of one James Smithson had been incorporated in an institute 'to promote science and the useful arts and to establish a national museum of history'. Belief was growing, belief in the virtue which lay in those accumulations of art and curiosities which men had brought together all over the world, if only that virtue could be made available to the common people who were already taking over the reins of power. But for a long time yet it seemed enough that the people were at last free to view collections of treasures which at one time had been seen only by the privileged few. The notion of mission had lost the urgency it had had in the days following the Great Exhibition, and became submerged in a new sort of collecting, this time with the aid of the public purse.

That collecting in itself is not enough has troubled many people in the museum profession, and their efforts to bring about revolutionary changes have had a great deal of success. They have recognized that if museums are to come alive and stay alive they must present more than collections: they must present ideas. It is not enough to permit the public to view vistas of stuffed animals.

15

Not that stuffed animals have not served us well, for many a fascinated small boy has sown the seeds for a subsequent distinguished career as a biologist by just staring at them on wet Saturday afternoons; but biology is far too basic a subject for us all, far too exciting, that we should be content with such casual and hit-or-miss recruitment to the ranks of its students. The impact made by rows of stuffed animals is nothing beside the impact which may be made by the imaginative presentation of biological ideas. Evolution is an obvious example. The story of the development of life on this earth from its first stirrings in the primeval mud to the complexities revealed by modern science is worthy of something more than humdrum, conventional display work and, in a great museum at least, should be carried out with appropriate grandeur of scale. This is not a matter of doing the visitor's work for him, as some would contend. It is to sweep him over the threshold into compellingly interesting, even awesome realms which he would not have discerned for himself hidden behind the stuffed carcase of a grizzly bear. Much of the evidence may be there for those with eyes to see in the traditional museum collections; but it is the duty of a curator to select, as a writer selects his words, and to devise a statement which will not only instruct, but first enthral. The lamellibranchs and the other denizens of the fossil galleries must be brought out of their obscurity to bear witness to the life that is gone, the lessons of environment be demonstrated, Mendl and Darwin given their places, and in the final phase the world of the living cell might be illustrated, as if under a gigantic microscope and in course of time maybe the secret of life itself . . .

These last words emphasize that the museum of ideas can have no finality. This is so much more than merely bringing a collection up-to-date, or of adding postscripts. The museum itself must be an organic whole, some part of it always in movement. It must be capable of changing with the times, with the needs of the times. A museum in which the sacrosanctity of the collections comes first is crushed by a millstone, incapable of radical change, and so far as the public is concerned its collections become less articulate as they increase, a barrier to enlightenment rather than an aid.

There is constant pressure today for the re-housing of museum collections, and several architects have turned to planning in this field; but though gloom and overcrowding and other past evils are disappearing, the dominant consideration is still usually the better display of 'the collections', where the aim should be to give expression to a theme or a complex of themes. It is true that some new architects and designers insist that the time has come for the curator to hand over his material to them for presentation since they, not he, are the experts in this field, but although this can result in spacious and tasteful displays and may come in for approving comment in the professional journals, fundamentally it shows no advance. The plan must be dictated by the man with the ideas. The first postulate is not: what have we got to house? It is: what do we want to say? For example, no subject has suffered more by meaningless clutter in museums than ethnography, and one new answer to the clutter is to dress the subject up in aesthetic poses and in the name of Art to demand obeisance to African idols stuck full of rusty nails—incidentally inflating their price in the 'art' market!—when all the time the real need is to sort out those rather baffling objects and give them meaning. This is not the place to get side-tracked, but when one thinks of the innumerable facets of ethnography—art, magic and beliefs, economics, technology, medicine, and so on— it grows clear that one must impose ideas if this extraordinary material is to acquire significance for the ordinary visitor.

Again, the current enthusiasm for industrial archaeology is a useful step in the march of conservation, but as conservation is only one of a museum's functions it must not be forgotten that what is needed is to bring technology into perspective by telling well the enthralling story of the evolution of tools from the stone artifact to the space-capsule, planned—shall we say?—as Lewis Mumford plans his books. Thus, as in *Technics and Civilisation*, it is not so much clocks which are important as the measurement of time, indeed all measurement; not so much engines as the harnessing of the power in steam or petrol-vapour or electricity. The conservation of old water-wheels on the site is commendable, but they need a context. Given such a context, either installed indoors, turning and dripping and clanking, or in an open-air museum, they can set right the misconceptions of the millions who think the Industrial Revolution began with James Watt. Specimens should not be exhibited because they happen to be there, but because they illustrate ideas.

17

Recently a writer in *Museum* said that science museums are tending to become science centres. It is quite possible in time that something like this will happen to all public museums, and that activities such as demonstrations and lectures, films, the convening of discussion-groups and conferences will become as important as the exhibits. We have come a long way from the day when the visitor to the museum was privileged and required to sign a visitors' book, yet if the barriers seem to have gone and the warders are less like policemen than they were—although in some museums in the United States they still carry guns on their hips!—there is a lingering air of aloofness in some at least of our museums, a tomb-like hush which indicates that the living, if they behave themselves, may only just be permitted to look upon the achievements of dead generations. The visitor has to be made to realize that the museum exists for him, not merely for an unseen priesthood of specialists, that it is something in which he himself can participate. Despite gun-packing warders, American museums do seem to have gone further than we have done towards the notion of a museum as a cultural centre. The museum over there in fact carries little of the off-putting public image, and even in New York a taxi-driver will chat familiarly about 'the Met.'. Museums are places where things happen.

I shall have things to say about the direction and staffing of museums later in this book, but I suspect that at this point the reader may be asking himself whether the museum of ideas does not imply an entirely new type of curator, a radical if not a revolutionary, at whose coming the pale, academic faces of existing staffs will grow yet paler. The popular concept of a museum curator does not, on the whole, fit the reality. Even when I say in later pages that planning the new museum may in itself be something of an act of artistic creation, I do not think it will scandalize more than a very few of those who were lately my colleagues. The museum of ideas is already coming into being, or is poised to do so, and it is only the slowness of the outside world to see the potentialities of museums which has held it back. However rich a collection may be, it has to be re-interpreted for every new generation, and by that I do not mean sand-blasting the facade of the building and redecorating the galleries. I mean taking a profound new look at the purpose of the institution, at the attitudes of the community and its needs, at methods whereby the gap

18

between may be bridged. Imagination, enthusiasm, understanding: all these have parts to play in stirring up again the ferment of creativity out of which most of our museums originally grew. When Oskar von Miller founded the Deutsches Museum he had a sort of epic vision of science and technology, and to me what he achieved has a Wagnerian quality, like a processional, now solemn and dramatic, now lyrical, his rather peremptory direction-signs forming a *leitmotif*, the inevitable pursuit of truth. By contrast, André Levcillé's Palais de la Découvérte pursues the same truths in a wholly Gallic way, its stated purpose to stimulate the visitor to explore 'the why and wherefore of things'. Both are essentially museums of ideas. Both have ceaseless change built into them. To present the world's masterpieces of art in the same challenging, disturbing way anew for each generation is, perhaps, not called for; and yet one is left with the uneasy feeling that one is evading a responsibility by thinking so. If art is an element essential to a full and happy life, then somehow it too may have to be re-interpreted for every successive age.

II The Monolithic Museum

'MONOLITHIC' HAS ACQUIRED a denigratory meaning, and it would be idle to pretend this is not the reason I have used it here; but monoliths have their appeal, and there is a case for massive concentration of material.

The argument dates a little. It belongs with nineteenth-century faith in encyclopaedic knowledge, when collecting and classifying material was the pathway to truth. It lingered on and lends real weight in the controversy over the British Museum site. It is a major part of the case for maintaining library and museum collections under one roof—more or less—that nowhere else in the world can a researcher, be he Karl Marx or an obscure delver into forgotten eccentricities of modes and manners, be so sure of getting what he wants with the minimum of effort. This argument is scouted by those who point out that in a computerized age a time is coming when information will be available at the press of a button, no matter where it is stored; but quite apart from the fact that we are still a long way from having a world dialling code system for information recovery, could such a system satisfy all scholars? No one has yet devised a computer which can be browsed through for unexpected things, or a recording bank which will enable a connoisseur to 'smell' the authorship of new material by means of his sixth sense. An institution like the British Museum—and in this respect one must bracket with it dozens of other great museums throughout the world—packs under its roof not only vast quantities of the raw material of scholarship and the books which are the scholar's tools, but also for consultation staff who are authorities in their various fields and intimately acquainted with the riches under their care. Whatever the arguments against the monolithic museum, to prise apart an organization of such formidable standing and proved value without such an investigation as would satisfy those most concerned would be irresponsible indeed, although sheer pressure on space may create an out-station, as in the case of the British Museum's ethnographical material.

A rather less obvious case for the monolithic museum, but one which has its points, is the argument of impact, impact on the public. Size itself is an impressive quality. Imhotep knew what he was doing when he built the Step Pyramid for Zoser. The modern argument against over-aweing visitors to museums is suspect in the light of the popularity of the gigantic in every age. Sheer size can achieve and sustain a power of arresting attention which outclasses all the gimmicks of the advertising expert. What you do with the attention when you have got it is another matter, but it is something to be able to command it just by existing on an enormous scale. Even the quantitative display has its advantages, and it is made possible only by possession of huge collections. Selective presentation, the 'star' piece spotlit in isolation, has its uses; but again and again I have proved to my own satisfaction that the lay public, far from being intimidated by mass display, dotes on it. The less casual visitor, the visitor who comes because he wants to find out something, also revels in quantity. The boy who has contrived to collect six or seven local species of butterfly, the amateur with a few modest pieces of porcelain, these are entranced by vistas of perfect specimens in wide variety. This is a different sort of impact, but it is as important as the impact on the casual visitor, because small-scale collectors are the museum's regular customers. For such people, a museum can no more be too massive than a vein can contain too much gold for a prospector.

There are other advantages in a monolithic museum, on the curatorial side, perhaps foremost among them the organization of staff and services. I have already referred to the authoritative role of the officers of an institution like the British Museum. This can only be developed to the full where there is staff in plenty to do the chores, whether professional ones of cataloguing and routine research and restoration, administrative ones of security, recruitment and office work, or those of direct service to the public in the form of display work on the galleries or educational schemes. The increased specialization and efficiency in the modern museum which are gradually producing a better image for the public are possible only through big increases in staff, and those are possible only in the larger institutions.

Not least of the arguments in favour of the very large museum is that it can sustain a visitor's interest over many visits without the repeated rearrangement which would be necessary in a smaller

21

place. The major problem in a local museum is that everybody knows what is in it. Unless it puts on special shows it will attract only strangers to the town. The museum of massive resources challenges the explorer's instinct. It also offers material to suit every taste and mood. This last may seem a curious point to make, but moods are an important element in deciding between interest or boredom in a museum visitor. Anyone of sensitive apprehension knows there are times when he can 'take' West African carvings and times when he cannot. On a day of November gloom he may want to escape to the elegance of eighteenth-century France or to the dream-world of Japanese *netsuké*. Revulsion against the commercialism of the streets outside may induce a longing for the timeless and the contemplative that will derive satisfaction from medieval stained glass or the serenely classical Buddha-figures of Gandhara. Disgust with a smug society may be forgotten in the awesome company of Maya sculpture. And so on . . . It is my belief that more people than might be imagined 'escape' into museums to satisfy a mood, as they may seek solace in a church, and if this is true it is an important social function, and there can be no question that the more wide-ranging and extensive the collections the more likely they are to find what they want. The little isolated figures of visitors seated, oblivious of the passing priest, under the soaring vaults of Beauvais or Canterbury cathedrals have their counterparts on the too-rare benches of our great museums; but the operative word is 'great', and if we were to rationalize and redistribute the wealth of those places it might well be that dispersal would dissipate the element of sanctuary.

However, the adjective I have used initially is not 'great' but 'monolithic'. Undoubtedly there has been growing a body of criticism of the heavy concentrations of material in a few large cities, with smaller towns and centres having to make do with little or nothing. In a sense it is reflected in the Arts Council policy of spending a higher proportion of available money on the provinces and on travelling facilities, and a great deal has been written and said about redistribution and about the need to put government money behind regional museums with first-class collections. Even in France, Malraux as Minister of Culture envisaged making Paris a little less the hub of all cultural affairs by creating centres in the major cities. Here London is just as dominant. The argument that disproportionate subsidies, in relation to population, spent on enterprises such as Covent Garden or the National Theatre are justified by their fertilizing opera or the drama throughout the country is unconvincing, and even less can one say that the remoter parts of England and Scotland benefit appreciably from the national institutions in London and Edinburgh. Monolithic concentrations serve only a small part of the community which maintains them through taxes.

But one fallacy must be nailed. The notion that 'surplus' material from the larger museums and galleries could by lavish redistribution enrich small museums up and down the land is as naive as the myth that the wealth of the rich would, if given to the poor, end poverty. Few museums resemble icebergs, with nine-tenths of their treasures out of sight, among art museums perhaps only those with departments of prints and drawings. Some have duplicates or near-duplicates which they would never miss— Dr. Alma S. Wittlin refers to 'hoards of duplicates in the cata-comb-like storage-rooms'—but not many art museums could mount from their reserve collections a display which would be more than a pale shadow of the display now in their public galleries. Nor are the quantity or quality of the reserve collections neces-sarily going to increase greatly in the future. The tradition that what the nation acquires is for ever, is breaking down. Most museums now have powers, with due safeguards, to dispose of material which they no longer need, even to use the proceeds to swell a little their all too meagre purchasing powers. There is a natural tendency for them to dispose of duplicate pieces first, and it will always be specimens of lesser quality which are parted with, but the tradition that it requires an Act of Parliament to dispose of anything is on its way out. What it all amounts to, however, is that even more in the future than now a redistribu-tion from the greater to the smaller museums would do little to make these latter more attractive and effective. An effective museum is not an inert collection of specimens, or even of master-pieces, and merely to add a few dozen new things from London's surplus to some provincial museum will not put that provincial museum on the map. If they were numbered in thousands in-stead of dozens there might be a case, but dozens at most is what it would be.

If I use the word monolithic in a disparaging sense it is be-cause those museums and galleries to which it applies are specially prone to inertia through their own overweightedness. As with the dinosaur, their very bulk makes it more difficult for them to adapt to a changing world. It is even possible for their staffs to become corrupted by their corpulence, to see virtue and take pride in increasing size. This is the miser's attitude, the attitude of the man who will part with nothing and puts it all in his attic in case he may find a use for it some day. Every curator should search his conscience about this, and do it ceaselessly. There is no hope for him as a museum administrator if he becomes the slave of acquisition because his obsession will stifle his capacity to serve either scholars or the community. His effective researches will end, he will write no papers for learned journals, he will have no time or patience for the humble public who want some elementary information about the things in his care. In this sense quite a small museum may become monolithic.

The real danger lies in the centralization of national effort in a small number of very large institutions. And I mean effort, rather than collections. A museum is to be rated by its effective impact on the community, not merely by the quantity or even quality of its contents. Perhaps it is unfair constantly to contrast our situation here with the situation in a supremely wealthy country like the United States, but the part played by the museum there in proliferating interest in the arts is by no means all a question of rich gifts from local millionaires. The Virginia Museum of Fine Arts in Richmond, for example, is far from extensive in the size of its collections, but it contrives to be a live cultural centre for the city and a focus for all the arts, including the drama, which it promotes in an excellently-equipped theatre. Other museums, such as the Baltimore Institute of the Fine Arts, are focal points for the teaching of art. Germany again, with her Staatsoper and Landesmuseum tradition, has a strongly decentralized culture-spread at a more sophisticated as well as at a folk level. New developments in places like Bonn and Mainz are not based on rich collections, except in the field of Rhenish antiquities, but they are carried out with professional finish on a basis of impeccable scholarship. Cologne, Stuttgart, Nuremburg are among many 'provincial' centres in West Germany where there are museums first-rate in every respect, and Munich of course can vie with any capital city in the world in this field. It is scarcely necessary to turn to Italy, but it should be stressed that curators in the smaller Italian cities are by no means content to rest on the laurels of their usually superb heritage but are often as eager to present their treasures well as are the most forward-looking of their colleagues in Rome or Florence. In those countries there is no domination by a few monolithic central institutions.

One aspect of such domination which has been called in question a few times in recent years is a certain tradition of the overriding right of acquisition of local finds by the central institutions at the expense of local interest: monolithic monopoly, as it might be called. When a rich hoard is discovered in this country it may or may not be declared treasure trove, but more often than not such 'trove' finds its way into one or another of the larger central museums. Protests at this practice are increasing. Sometimes they have a political tinge. Often they are fanned by the local press, not above cashing in on easily-roused indignation. What the protesters are ignorant of or forget is that there are two well-founded reasons for the practice. One is that many more people have access to the material, including scholars, and that the new finds may be examined in the context of comparable objects. The other reason is that only the large central institutions are equipped to restore and preserve the finds and to maintain them safely under the proper conditions. Neither reason is to be lightly swept aside. It is quite true that an object can acquire greater meaning when seen among its peers; and restoration is a process which has to be followed up by at least a long period of watchful care, and with precious materials there is the question of security, which is no longer merely a question of fitting a good lock to a glass case. Sentiment, therefore, in the short term at least, may be a dangerous prompter in the controversies which have arisen over the destination of treasure trove.

Nevertheless, the practice of depositing centrally all the choicest local finds needs to be reviewed. I am thinking not so much of rendering the central museums less monolithic as of building up the status of local museums. Collecting policy in local museums is something which I will take up later, but the reflection of local culture is a corner-stone of policy, and if this is reduced to the level of the second-rate and the visitor has to be referred to London, Edinburgh or Cardiff for some treasure which would have changed the whole aspect of the local picture, then something needs to be done about it. As to the argument about the convenience of scholars, I have small patience with it. The foundations on which most scholars build today were laid by men and women who thought nothing of getting where they needed to go by brake, gig, bicycle or on their own two feet, and if the resources of modern transport are not good enough for the new generation then I can only say that scholarship will be the worse for such feebleness of spirit. Even a scholar should gain from seeing a work against the background native to it.

But the main burden of the case for retaining part at least of a rich find in the museum nearest to the place in which it was found is that to dispossess communities of such things robs them of some of their heritage, and so diminishes them. It makes the task of the local museum harder, both in maintaining interest in the community and in attracting visitors from other places. Without denying the need for fully representative collections in the great national and municipal museums, I would make a strong plea for the retention in regional and local museums of enough rich material to enable, first, the resident to be alive to the importance of his heritage and, second, the visitor to appreciate the achievements and history of the district. The Roman Wall would mean little to the average tourist without the concentrations of legionary material at Chester and Newcastle, and the ancient culture of Strathmore would be lost on all but a few without the little museums at Meigle and St Vigeans. Even France, so conscious of the advantages of centralization, has left the treasure of Vix in the tiny village museum at Châtillon-sur-Seine. If the monolithic monopoly too often overrides the claims of such places as these, it will be to the gradual impoverishment of the country.

I would add to this a rider about church and country house. It is one of the tragedies of our times that economic pressures are breaking up the pattern of our cultural heritage, and it is sometimes argued that funds should be given to our great museums to 'save' the contents of our country houses and even at times our churches when these are forced on to the open market. It is true there should be readier means of retaining significant things threatened with export, but it is of the first importance to keep such things, if it be possible, under the roofs which have sheltered them for centuries. Most of our great museums have treasures enough to serve their purposes: the rest of our treasures should, where they can, be kept in their contexts. It is especially deplor-

26

able that churches should feel constrained to part with their plate or fittings to meet the costs of maintenance or of expanding their social services, but this is happening on an increasing scale. The bronze lectern which went recently from England to an American museum made the headlines, but there are many lesser cases which do not. When I have been approached about the possibility of 'saving' a service of Communion plate by acquiring it for my own museum I have felt no delight at the opportunity. It is of course argued that a new church hall is of more value to the parish than a set of silver vessels normally kept in the bank vaults; but the retort to this is that men of good faith three centuries ago deprived themselves that the church might have its goodly plate, and that it shows a poor spirit for their counterparts of today to build a hall out of their predecessors' generosity instead of their own. And it is far preferable to see these beautiful things displayed in an elegant case in the church, if it can be done with reasonable safety, rather than consign them to the anonymity of a great museum. Where security is concerned, the answer may lie in the institution of church treasuries, such as many large churches abroad and a growing number in England already possess. My own Livery company, the Worshipful Company of Goldsmiths, has done much to make these possible, and in the case of Winchester, for example, plate from several churches in the diocese has been brought together in conditions of security.

III 'Treasure' Hunting

ANTIQUES ARE BIG money. At one time museums did not have to think so much in terms of the art market, partly because taxation had not then checked the generosity of donors, but the situation is now very different and the museum director more and more is being forced to become a business man. In this chapter I want to say something about museums in relation to the art market; but since the nation's treasures, its cultural capital, are coming under the same sort of threat as its material wealth, I propose also to discuss whether or not museums should have a part in retaining and preserving them.

Commercial trafficking in works of art is by no means a new thing. For some readers, this may seem too obvious to need saying; but in my experience an overwhelming majority of people believe the international art market is a relatively recent phenomenon and that the large-scale selling of treasures goes back no more than a few generations. To those still under such a delusion, I recommend Germain Bazin's recent volume, *The Museum Age*. There, I will not say in a nutshell but in very readable form, may be found a record of more than two thousand years of the buying and selling of treasures, and of how this traffic has helped to create some of the great museums of the old and new worlds. Cynical depredation is not a thing of this twentieth century. Even tombs have been plundered and temples and churches spoiled for quick profits in all ages. Art has never been sacrosanct.

It could well be argued, however, that never previously has there been the machinery to compare with what we have today, both for preserving our old buildings and ancient monuments *in situ* and for maintaining barriers to stem the outflow of masterpieces from one country to another. France, always conscious of the dignity of her place in the art world, has for generations, perhaps ever since the Revolution, striven to stop the outflow of

28

native works of art and to buy back what she could. Italy, after centuries of spoliation, is now as alert as France to prevent further losses. In the United Kingdom, the Ancient Monuments authorities have scheduled and preserved thousands of structures ranging from remote, vestigial sites to historic abbeys and castles, and in the Export of Works of Art Committee, working with the Board of Trade, there is a means of checking at least some of our losses through the market. Even the under-developed countries are no longer quarries freely open to the collectors and museums of richer and more powerful peoples. But in spite of all that is being done, the situation is far from reassuring to anyone who knows what is really happening.

For years there has been an ominous new element in the art market, or perhaps one should say a rise to dominance of an element which has always been present. In all ages art treasures have been investments, but in the past they attracted mainly genuine lovers of the arts or wealthy men who wanted to acquire culture, or the appearance of it. Today those treasures are taking their place beside common stocks and shares, are being bought and sold by people who care nothing for the arts or even for the prestige bestowed by possession of masterpieces. Thousands must have responded with delight to Mr L. J. Olivier's trenchant letter to *The Times* (22nd October 1968) on the subject of '*The Times*-Sotheby Index'. Slashing the commercial art market, he ends by saying, 'One day, please God, the tide will turn. The air-conditioned vaults of philistine businessmen will be broken open and the contents expropriated and your wretched art journalists will be stoned to death with fake Etruscan bronzes. In the meantime, a curse on your loathsome percentages and despicable graphs, and shame on you, Sir.'

It is a materialistic age, but this surge of commercialism in the art market puts the art museums and galleries in a far worse position than they have ever been in, in spite of the improvement in their financial backing. This is more especially true if we look upon museums as 'collections', an interpretation of their function which I criticized in the first chapter; but in so far as all museums must, in some degree, collect, the new situation is an unhappy one. Art treasures, whether paintings, sculptures or *objets d'art*, in an inflationary economy such as we have to suffer, are as near as possible to perfect investments, better even than

B

land, the value of which may be subject to the whims and vagaries of planners, local and ministerial. They are gilt-edged stocks with a built-in steady capital appreciation which, in some categories at least, may well double their value every five years or so. The investor in this field, in fact, if he is sure of what he is buying, comes as near as may be to knowing he cannot lose.

Museums, therefore, are facing a situation in which they have to compete for their stock-in-trade against buyers to whom their annual purchase-grants are mere chicken-feed. To acquire the Leonardo cartoon for the nation was far beyond the means of the National Gallery, and an appeal had to be launched to the public to make the purchase possible. This is an extreme case; but every month, even every week, lesser masterpieces are lost by one museum or another because the museums have not the means to bid for them. The curator cannot turn to the authorities with the plea that art is as good an investment for public as for private money, because the treasures which find their way into public museums are meant to stay there. It is no real consolation to the Treasury or to city treasurers to know they are sitting on an appreciating capital which they can never realize. It is certainly some small consolation to the curator to be able to urge collectors not to realize their money by selling their collections unless they have to and thus to help stem a little the outflow from the country; at the same time he knows those collections are unlikely ever to come his way, however long he may wait. In the United States, the era of benevolent patronage has been extended by enlightened tax concessions, but there is nothing quite comparable in this country, and the day of the Wallaces and the Saltings and the Burrells is at an end. There may still be reasons weighty enough to persuade rich men of good will to bequeath their old masters to a public gallery, and indeed this part of their estate will be exempt from death duties if they so do. However, a painting which may well double its value in a decade is not lightly to be parted with.

Does this mean that museums should be provided with perpetually inflating purchase-grants, instead of quinquennial or other long-term adjustments to their grants, to enable them to compete successfully in the art market? Some of those lately my colleagues in the profession would, I believe, almost go so far as to say they should. In my own view, and I am sure in the views of most curators, it would be quite wrong. Anything which adds to the crazy momentum of inflation must, in principle, be unsound, but apart from this, any museum's purchase needs are erratic and obviously are influenced by what is offered on the market. There will always be masterpieces which, for one reason or another, simply have to be acquired for the nation or for a particular community, but the whole approach to public 'collecting' needs to be reviewed, which is what the first chapter of this book was about. This does not mean that the purchase-grants of our museums are generally satisfactory. No grant which can be exhausted for several years by a single purchase could be called satisfactory. Grants for museums in this country at present are pitifully inadequate even for modest targets. At the end of each year for the past thirty-odd years I have sometimes marvelled at the showing made not only by my own institution but far more by those of some of my colleagues, and I could only conclude we were somehow endowed with a little of the spirit of the miracle of the loaves and fishes. Though of course careful scrutiny shows that few even of the more vital gaps are ever filled. If we may have the chance of a bargain here, or there receive a special grant towards an unexpected acquisition progress towards our various goals is a sprawling, unbalanced and frustrating business. There can be no question, then, that grants be put on what some might call a realistic basis; but—and it is a fundamental 'but'—first there should be a radical review of acquisition policy, not only in each individual museum but in museums as a whole. Inevitably purchase-grants must tend overall to increase substantially every year while we continue to have an economy which accepts perpetual devaluation of the currency, and there is also the factor of the increasing rarity of almost everything in the art market, which operates like Tarquin's purchase of the Sibylline Books. On the other hand, any national acquisition policy must anticipate something like an eventual approach to satiety, certainly in many sectors of a museum. Normally there will always be room for improvement in the collections of any museum, however vast, but there is no good reason why this process should not involve disposal as well as acquisition.

I mentioned in passing at the beginning of the chapter that directors of museums were being forced into the role of business men, a state of affairs in which the inflationary art market is undoubtedly a major factor. This in itself seems to me to be most unfortunate. In some places, perhaps notably in the United States, it seems to be quite widely accepted, and it is not unknown for a director to be recruited mainly on the strength of his capacity to raise and manage money. Some of the greatest directors in the past, not in art museums only, have had a masterful way with millionaires and industrialists, and if they have the burning zeal and idealism to convince such hardheaded people it is a valuable quality. It should not, however, be the primary quality needed. Some men can take these things in their stride, but if the special gifts and judgement needed to project and promote the idea of a great museum are warped by too-pressing financial frustrations there will be little real progress.

So we come to the other side of the problem raised by the high market value of art treasures: the preservation of our cultural heritage, and the threat imposed by the export drive. How, in fact, does our birthright measure up in importance to our society against the mess of pottage; and if it is important, do our museums, with their special knowledge, have a responsibility for the preservation of it?

It is neither practicable nor reasonable to oppose a certain export of native cultural work, and it is obviously in the interest of international understanding. I am, however, one of those who believe that one cannot uproot art from its natural setting and hope completely to understand it, and that if it is to have its full impact one must be forced to see and experience it in the country of its origin. It is no doubt satisfactory for Americans to be able to study French silver in great detail in the remarkable collection in the Metropolitan Museum, but this does not compensate for the disappointment of students visiting some important French provincial museums to find virtually no silverware at all. Even more disappointing it is to visit great and beautiful houses which prove to be empty shells, as with some of the chateaux of the Loire. The question of the country-house museum will be discussed elsewhere, but I will say now that in my view the country house has a great advantage over the conventional museum in providing the right environment for furnishings and not the house alone, but its contents, should be scheduled for preservation, if necessary at state or local authority expense, in cases where this seems justified. It is an area very vulnerable to the depredations of the antiques export trade. In my own lifetime I have seen more treasures than I can count disappear from houses which I know.

Britain is still among the more fortunate countries in respect of her country houses. They have never been sacked of their furnishings and plate and table-wares as the houses of France were at the Revolution, but the social revolution here will be just as thorough in its effects if steps are not taken now to stem its depredations. What the Revolution accomplished in France in a few years the incidence of death duties is doing systematically over a longer period in Britain. Some great houses have fought off the threat by opening to the public on a commercial basis, others have been taken over by the National Trusts, a very few of them accepted in lieu of death duties and given into the stewardship of the Trusts. However, the contents of our old houses represent hundreds of millions of pounds of capital. Efforts to coax or force this money back into circulation are ceaseless. It is not enough to introduce small-scale mitigating action to alleviate the effects of legislation which in itself is hostile to the long-term interests of the community.

Apollo magazine, in its issue of June 1968, printed an important editorial comment on this problem. It was a defence of the position of the private collector and of his service to society, so much so indeed that the writer felt he had to make it clear that he had no hostility to 'the public institutions'; but the public institutions, if they are to be worthy of the name, cannot be indifferent to anything which will diminish the national heritage, and the 'dismemberment' of 'capitalistic independence' involves no simple transfer of paper wealth from private pockets to the coffers of the state. As the article points out, dismemberment which begins with taxes on private assets, augmented by devaluation, could end by striking at the whole of our artistic life and bring about a collapse of the art market too. And as far as the private collector is concerned, the article rightly stresses that 'the existence of as many collectors as possible secures the creation of an informed body of opinion which can evaluate the policies of galleries and museums. Moreover, collectors are often in a position to explore unfashionable territories which may not at a particular moment be sought after by the institutions.' In-

33

deed, in collecting, the private sector and the public are by no means opposed and hostile to one another. We know well enough that preservation of our cultural heritage is one of the functions of museums. Any threat to any part of this heritage is therefore a matter of concern for our museums. It is one of the main purposes of this book to emphasize that museums are no mere repositories, but are institutions with several positive functions, and one of these should be—and not infrequently is—to be watch-dogs against attempts to erode our treasures, no matter in whose keeping they be.

There are several ways in which museums are called upon, from time to time, to give evidence or even judgement about the fate of a work of art. Probably the most frequent is consultation as to whether or not a licence for export should be issued by the Board of Trade. This is an invaluable safeguard, much appreciated by specialists in the museums; but there are many loopholes which should be stopped, and some of us would be happy to see a much more ruthless machinery for retaining outstanding pieces, especially those by British artists and craftsmen. One notable product of a Scottish goldsmith which should never have been allowed to leave Scotland, despite the dollars it brought, some years ago escaped the net simply because it had been owned or part-owned for a few years by someone in the United States. It is impossible to believe a French piece would have left France, or an Italian piece Italy, by such a quaint loophole in the law. There are of course those who maintain that the need for dollars must outweigh considerations of keeping our artistic heritage intact: their argument can be met on its own level by pointing out that one does not dispose of steadily appreciating capital except in desperation.

Another, much greater, loophole in our defences is that the mesh of the net is too large to catch smaller things which may yet be invaluable, even unique. £4,000 is at present the minimum value for any work of art if it is to be considered for refusal of an export licence. The museums have repeatedly pointed out that pieces with a much lower market value, for example some archaeological objects, may nevertheless be unique. True, no one could hope to devise machinery to scrutinize every work of art or of fine craftsmanship which finds its way into the export pipe-line; but the appropriate museum should always have the last word in any case which comes to its knowledge, provided it is willing and in a position to make the purchase. The basis for a system of safeguarding our heritage of art treasures might well be a comprehensive list of master-works in private possession which under no circumstance would receive an export licence; such a list to be drawn up quite irrespective of monetary values. A list of this kind would not only help to safeguard the country's treasures: it would also do much to eliminate situations liable to breed hostility between the authorities here and those foreign collectors who, in good faith, now acquire important pieces in the British market only to be refused permission to take them out of the country.

Even this proposal unfortunately could do nothing to stem the drain of minor antiques and paintings which is steadily robbing our smaller houses, even our cottages, of much of their interest. For years certain dealers have been combing the countryside, offering £5 for a grandfather clock of perhaps the early nineteenth century, confident in the knowledge they can get anything from £50 to £100 for it in the right market, and I have seen pantechnicons drawn up outside their shops week after week with crates labelled with destinations in North or South America. This sort of thing never hits the headlines because journalists are rarely interested in art which has no big price tag attached. But this is diminishing our heritage even more surely than the loss of the occasional masterpiece of international repute. In terms of cultural wealth, the masterpiece is only the peak of a pyramid, and if the pyramid collapses, that masterpiece may look a sorry relic indeed lying in a bare desert. Traditionally museums are not interested in such minor things. Already they are becoming more interested. Some of them are even acquiring Victorian bric-à-brac. But the new museums must acquire also vigilance and a positive policy about the depletion of the environment in which they work.

Sky-rocketing market values of works of art unhappily have played havoc with true values in the eyes of the public, and sometimes one wonders if the judgement of some of the museums themselves have not been distorted by this. Prices in the art market are not always regulated by the factor of artistic merit. It is difficult for a serious art historian not to be disturbed by the relative market prices of certain modern paintings, for example,

35

when compared with the prices of paintings of much earlier times. It is possible to acquire an exquisite seventeenth-century piece, or an even earlier work, for a fraction of the price of an Impressionist landscape. The public of course pays most attention to the things which fetch the big prices, as the Chairman of Sotheby's himself has stated (B.B.C., 4th February 1972). One may therefore often anticipate queues for shows of the works of certain contemporaries who, one suspects, will not be called masters in a hundred years, whereas works of indubitable merit which have withstood the test of time may achieve only meagre attendances. This makes rather a nonsense of the function of museums to promote the real 'treasures' for the less discerning eye. Sometimes I go so far as to wonder if a museum should be permitted to spend public money on works which have not survived what, in the parlance of industrial disputes, might be called a 'cooling-off period'. I will return to this briefly in Chapter V.

The dealer wields far greater power in the art world than does the curator. No one who has negotiated with them could have anything but the greatest respect for the knowledge and connoisseurship of the specialist staffs of the great art dealers and auctioneers. Indeed, I believe that the young trainee of a famous London auction house who, unaware of my profession, insisted that the apprenticeship in such a firm is a more effective preparation for connoisseurship than the equivalent years in a national museum was not quite so rash as he seemed, since the discipline of staking big money on an opinion is no doubt more testing than staking a budding academic reputation; and I am certainly not in favour of the one-time unwritten law that discouraged keepers and assistant-keepers of the national museums from indulging in private collecting. But having said this, I must come back to the fundamental fact that it is the first instinct of the curator to conserve and of the dealer to deal. None who feels concern for the preservation of our cultural heritage but must have a sense of foreboding over the systematic squeezing of the country by the big auction houses and their establishment of agents far from London to encourage people to ransack their attics and to cream off anything that is worth while to the London mart. However knowledgeable and skilled and scholarly the art market experts may be, in the last resort they are helping to destroy our real wealth; and as we come nearer to scraping the bottom of the barrel, and in its desperation the art market exploits everything from Victoriana to model locomotives, the need for museums to put their weight behind a drastic effort to safeguard us from the mad treasure-hunt becomes more urgent.

IV A Museum is not a Building

MUSEUM THINKING has nearly always begun with the building. When anyone, be it a philanthropist or a public authority, decided to have a museum, the proposal has tended from a very early stage to crystallize as an architectural concept. Over the past hundred years or so this has materialized as a temple of the muses or as something which is neither quite a cathedral nor yet a town hall, because such forms seemed appropriate to the storage of publicly-owned relics of great value and fitted the architects' notions of a 'prestige' building in a civic milieu. The classical porticos of the British Museum and the National Gallery can be seen performing the same function in half the major cities of the world, the alternative being an equally formidable romanticism such as we have in the Natural History Museum in London, the Deutsches Museum in Munich or Nordiska Museet in Stockholm.

This image of the traditional museum has not been drawn merely so that it can be withered with scorn. In the chapter on the monolithic museum I declared there was much to be said for monoliths. There is something to be said also for classical porticos, and for the vaguely reverential attitude induced by the precincts of what seems to be a temple or a repository of temporal power. Reverence is an attitude in diminishing supply, and we are not encouraged to be awestruck either by promoters of the arts today or even by our interpreters of scientific progress. There are ways of creating a proper spirit of anticipation other than penetration of a solemn neo-classic barrier set between the museum and the workaday world, but at least there is as good a case for retaining such a barrier as for pulling it down.

What we have to be vigilant against is thinking of museums primarily in terms of buildings. We must cease to build our museums from the outside in. This may seem an entirely unnecessary warning in an age when functionalism in architecture has been preached since the day when Corbusier first claimed that a house was a machine for living in; but, in fact, in spite of all the preaching, in spite of the seductive, glossy magazines, houses have tended to become more machine-like and less and less suitable for ordinary mortals to live in, unless living is to be interpreted as providing house-room for the products of the hire-purchase firms. The needs and wishes of the individual house-owner count for less and less. The majority of citizens have to be content with the meagre possibilities of the housing estate or the high-rise flat. For most of us the house has literally become a machine for living in, although the agent probably advertises it euphemistically as a 'home'. The same danger threatens the personal needs of our museums and galleries. Prior consultation may be never-ending and briefing sessions legion, but not all those procedures will effectively save the New Museum from being anything but what the architect thinks it should be, and even those architects who now specialize in museum work tend to impose their concepts on the concepts of their clients even at the risk of interfering with the basic functions of the institution. I recall, for example, an internationally-famous architect who objected to the introduction of a key-exhibit around which a whole gallery revolved on the ground that it interfered with his fenestration. The demand for museum modernization inevitably in this specialist age has created a supply of specialist architects and designers who are developing a *mystique* of their own. The *mystique* has already accumulated an array of stock theories and answers to problems, and this is making its mark on the contemporary museum just as surely as did the temple-of-the-muses school in the nineteenth century. However successful some of their early work may have been— and there are some very good new museums up and down the world today—the museum least of all public buildings can afford to be shaped according to formulæ, which will again set the seal of death on institutions which are only now learning how to come alive.

Even admirable beliefs about flexibility, adaptability or extroversion may rapidly crystallize into theories which impose an architectural solution too early in the planning of a new museum. Obsession with the 'evil' of nineteenth-century over-crowding has encouraged a sort of open-plan, glass-and-concrete style in which wide courtyards, vistas and water-features in themselves become an obsession and exhibits are hard to find. These light and airy buildings may be as inhibiting for works of art as are any of the museum buildings we have inherited from the past. Indeed the museum director or designer who is presented with one of those airy buildings may be less free to contrive the presentation of his themes than if he had a series of gloomy halls and corridors to work with, surroundings from which he can at least exclude the outside world in order to create a world of his own devising.

In Mr Michael Brawne's interesting survey, *The New Museum*, one feels from page to page a growing new architectural domination of the museum idea. One of the best examples of this domination in an early stage is the famous Solomon R. Guggenheim Museum in New York. This is a characteristically protean piece by Frank Lloyd Wright which neither fits into the rather gracious frontages of old Fifth Avenue, already regarded by discriminating New Yorkers as 'period', nor yet into the needs of a gallery for the display of paintings. The architect claimed for it that it would be proportioned to the human scale, and that it would produce 'a new unity between beholder, painting and architecture'. In fact, the architecture is all, not visually only but totally, for the downward spiralling of the galleries gently but inexorably propels the visitor toward the exit however great the appeal of the exhibits he is passing by. Even where the building itself is acceptable as a distinguished piece of architecture, as with Mies van der Rohe's Cullinan Hall of the Museum of Fine Arts at Houston, Texas, what we are given is a beautiful environment into which the curator may fit such paintings or sculpture as are appropriate. Exhibits are secondary. The concept is the architect's, not the curator's, however happy the curator may be with it. Here is one of the dangers of the open competition, because however carefully they may study the requirements, competing architects must commit themselves to paper long in advance, often without close knowledge of the site and the needs of the clients, and their submissions are judged probably by a committee, distinguished no doubt but without any responsibility for creating the museum that is to be. The result is likely to be a drawing-board museum. It has happened with many of the new museums both in Europe and the United States.

What, then, is a museum if it is not a building?

Ideally the director of any museum, great or small, should have in him an element of the creative artist. Basically, of course, he will be a scholar with a generous share of administrative ability developed in his own field over many years; but the special quality without which he will be doing little more than nominally filling the office is a compound of the powers of imagination, interpretation and steadfast dedication. Without this sort of direction no museum, however richly endowed, will be anything more than a collection. In short, the ideal museum in a sense is a work of art in its own right, whether its field be art or science. This assertion may evoke protest from the ranks of our curators; but in emphasizing the need for creative directorship I am in no way diminishing the need for those academic and curatorial skills on which the reputation of our great museums so largely rests. What we have to recognize is that unless the material on which those curating skills are exercised can be enlisted more fully into the service of society it is doubtful if even the present cost to the public purse is justified. Certainly much of it already serves society without ever being exposed to public view, by contributing to knowledge, but this sort of work needs only storage and laboratories, and the museum idea is something else.

The most positive purpose of the museum, where the man in the street is concerned, is to stimulate curiosity, pleasure, even awe by confrontation with the works of nature and of man, through this to rouse a hunger for knowledge and to give guidance about how it can be satisfied. To do this for visitors who, for the most part, are essentially casual is a challenge. It is a challenge which can be met successfully only by men or women who themselves feel keenly the significance of an artifact or a work of nature and who have the ability to transmit their feeling to others. And the head of a museum must be similarly conscious of the total potential of the material under his direction and be able and determined to use it not merely against ignorance but in the face of indifference. There is something epic in this challenge. I doubt if it can be met as it should be except by someone aware of it as a drama in which he must be a protagonist.

At this point a moment's thought will show how crippling to

the emerging idea of a museum it may be to put too much of the responsibility too early in the hands of the architect. I do not mean that the architect should not be associated with the planning of the museum until the director has finalized his requirements—this would be ridiculous; but it must be understood that the architect's function is an enabling one, not an initiating one, and the practice of sending architects on expensive 'educational' tours of foreign museums to collect tips on museum planning is somewhat naïve. Study of other museums is essential, obviously, for anyone engaged in planning a new museum, but this should be done over a long period so that impacts may recede from the foreground of thought, otherwise the result may be little more than a series of *pastiches*. The mistakes of others may be more useful guidelines than their achievements.

Here I must elaborate a little on something touched on in the introductory chapter. A museum is not a building but an idea, or it may be a complex of ideas. The exhibits, even the building itself, are part of the process of materialization. They are means of expression. Through them above all, rather than through labels or sound-tracks, the creator of the museum is rendered articulate. One of the great dangers in all museums is ossification, or perhaps one should say hardening of the arteries. This sets in as soon as the displays cease to put over to the visitor something of the interest and energy out of which they were conceived. Inevitably in the course of time this happens to all displays. What is exciting to one generation may be matter-of-fact to the next, and although great works of art or of nature are everlasting in their appeal, approach and context change and they have to be presented again in a new way. Nothing will more certainly condemn a museum to rapid ossification than to commit every section of it from the start, with structural treatments so permanent that nothing short of demolition can change them. There are exceptions. There are certain masterpieces or groups of masterpieces, such as the Elgin Marbles, which call for appropriate settings on such a scale that they cannot be reconstituted every twenty or thirty years and which therefore seem to commit the building or a part of it permanently; but such exceptions are few, and even those few should not be completely sacrosanct. It is the idea behind everything which in the final consideration must be the determining factor, and ideas are

42

never static and final. Even in the most permanent displays there should be room for an element of 'liquidity'—to use the financial term—so that there is something in reserve for response to changing needs. The more rigidly conceived the building, the less room there is in it for the play of new ideas, and if the concept is that of a strong-minded architect, as in the case of the Guggenheim, museum directors and staff are presented with what is virtually a prison. It may be an elegant and impressive prison, but that is not much consolation to the inmates if they want freedom to express their ideas.

Already it has been mentioned that open-plan buildings may also be inhibiting. At first sight they seem to be the answer not only to overcrowding but to the prior commitment of which I have complained. They seem to say: 'Here is all the space you want, all the light, with no predisposing environment—now get on with it, place your exhibits as you want them!' Indeed in many cases they do prove to be the answer to the problem. Yet at the risk of seeming perverse I must add they are by no means always the answer. Agoraphobia is as distressing as claustrophobia. Olympia may be an environment inviting to a circus manager, but not many museum directors would find it had much appeal. Most exhibits need a special relationship with their setting, and exhibits of the quality and importance normally associated with museums need a setting which is something more than a perfunctory piece of decor. In short, we are back to my contention that not every director is likely to be happy about taking over a building devised for him by someone else, however expert, and however neutral and accommodating the design.

It need hardly be said, of course, that as a rule this is not how museums get built. Requirements of director and staff are sought at an early stage in the proceedings, often in great detail, and steering committees are set up which meet at intervals until the whole thing is completed. Such at least is my own experience. However, if my theory that a museum is a work of art in its own right is to be maintained; if, that is, it is to be the elegant embodiment of the ideas of a creative and perhaps forceful personality, accepted procedures are fraught with frustrations. The client-architect relationship could work very well in an expansive age such as the eighteenth century, when the client was wealthy and he and the architect, scarcely separated by a barrier of professionalism, probably shared the same grandiose concepts of what a building should look like. The visionary client sometimes managed to have his way even in museum building earlier in the present century. With massive industrial support behind him, Oskar von Miller in 1903 was able to launch his Deutsches Museum in Munich as if it were some technological epic, and the same sort of commanding patronage made possible the reconstruction of Colonial Williamsburg in the 1920s, when John D. Rockefeller Jr. underwrote the dream of the Reverend W. A. R. Goodwin. Today visionaries have a hard time of it when their visions need big money. They have to convince so many people over so long a period that, unless they are very tough, their vision in the long run begins to flicker and grow dim. They find they have to compromise to get anything done at all. The fundamentals of the building will be determined in far too high a degree by the architects, who in turn will be influenced by the planning authority and perhaps by such consultative bodies as the Royal Fine Art Commission and the Standing Commission on Museums and Galleries.

Of course, to some extent management by committee is inevitable where the spending of public money is concerned. No one can look for largesse on the scale needed to achieve a great public building without strings attached. Nor can even the most autocratic director expect to impose whatever he wills upon the environment. There must be safeguards, financial and social. It is, however, ultimately only the director and his staff who will make a success of the new museum, and it is essential that accountants and architects are aligned on his side and not against him. By this I am not suggesting that responsible accountants or architects would deliberately frustrate the museum director, but rather that their part in the materialization of his ideas tends to come at too late a stage and that he finds himself brought back to earth rather rudely at times when his feet should have been firmly planted on it all the time. Most directors are academics. They may know what they want, but without knowing the practicalities of how to get it. If their ideas are to be properly clothed in the new building and not merely put into something ready made, if in fact it is to be the building which is tailored and not the ideas, then specialists such as architects and even accountants should be helping with the evolution of the ideas

44

from the start. This might seem to be an argument for having an architect permanently on the staff in the case of a great museum. This I am sure would be a mistake, because an architect with the quality of vision that is needed would in time find it a myopic existence. The answer may well be to develop the display side of the museum's activities to such a pitch of professional efficiency that the museum itself becomes completely articulate in the field of making its ideas architecturally viable, so that when the stage is reached for bringing in consultants any communication gap between museum and architect narrows to a minimum. If the museum can carry the materialization of its ideas to a stage when their practicability is beyond doubt, and at the same time be able to discuss them with the architect in his own language, then there is no reason why the client-architect relationship should not become a real marriage.

Display departments are relatively new features of museums, in the United Kingdom at least. However, they are already beginning to achieve some success in influencing the interior layout of new buildings, if nothing more. In the case of my own museum, the development of an introductory hall of biology on new and exciting lines was realized probably only because of the existence of a young but eager display department. The original idea was the result of discussion between two or three geologists and biologists of the senior staff, and by living with this idea and its promoters over a period of a year or two the head of the display department was able to shape it into something not less but more exciting than the first concept. Further, the scale model and working drawings he was able to make of the project were of a standard acceptable to the architects. Indeed, they were impressed, and even excited. Inevitably a point was reached when the architects felt their importance to the scheme had shrunk a little. Their reaction was to say: 'We want no model or working drawings, only your requirements—leave the solution to us.' But when the smoke of contention cleared they were found to have accepted the scheme in its fundamentals as given to them and to be discovering new ways of exercising their expertise by developing and refining the scheme. The architects' shouldering of the heavier problems of construction in turn freed the designer to concentrate on detail. Thus the building—or, to be precise, in this case a reconstructed interior—never went out

45

of the control of those who thought up the original idea and became an expression of that idea, not a constriction placed upon it.

The importance of not thinking of a new museum project initially in terms primarily of a building becomes more manifest every year. The museum concept is changing all the time, and although the housing of material collections obviously is basic to much of the thought and discussion given to the subject, there are so many other aspects to a modern museum. Education and amenities, once grudgingly allotted such little space as might be left over from the conservation and display of material, now occupy the very forefront in planning some of our new museums. Publication kiosks, formerly tucked into dark corners, now go hand-in-hand with the sale of reproductions and sometimes— especially in the United States—have become big business. Temporary exhibitions, once pushed into whatever space could be found without disturbing the permanent collections, now demand a place in the sun, with costly equipment and lighting. 'Friends' organizations, which already receive special consideration across the Atlantic, may well merit increasing priority of treatment here also, with reading-rooms and rest-rooms, possibly even their own cafeterias. Lectures and films are growing in importance, with a vast potential usefulness in enlarging the dimension of the museum collections by animating them and setting them in their own proper environments, and the public will not accept standards in these things which fall below those they are accustomed to in the commercial cinema. To these may be added the planetarium, the climaterium, and other sophisticated means of projecting and explaining new avenues of exploration both of the world and of space. Such are accepted adjuncts of the museum on the Continent and in America. A case may be made out for a museum theatre, for the drama has many points of contact with the other arts, and a museum theatre operates with notable success for example at Richmond, Virginia. Then again, on the directly educational side there is a need for classrooms and demonstration laboratories, to say nothing of rooms where children and students may eat without either making a nuisance of themselves in the public galleries or blocking the restaurants. As the reserve collections grow so also do the opportunities for advanced-level study and research. It is no longer enough just to admit students to the store-areas under supervision, for this activity should become more and more an extension of their university studies, and properly-equipped accommodation must be provided. In short, a museum is now much more than an institution housing collections relating to the arts and sciences, and to give it any form expressive of such an out-dated concept is to prejudice its development. A museum is a presence in the community, constantly changing in response to the needs of that community, and to think of it in terms of a building, however fine and prestigious, is wrong.

V Taking Museums Seriously

MUSEUMS ARE probably taken rather more seriously than they were half a century ago, but they have still a long way to go before they find their proper place in the scheme of things. The museum profession and everyone associated with it in advisory capacities have expended much thought and effort to bring order into something which verged upon chaos, but in spite of this museums count for much less than they should. Their functions and potentialities are hardly understood at all by politicians, administrators, economists and those professional and business men who determine our scale of values in public affairs. 'Museum' continues to be a derisory byword in public speeches for anything that is out of date. The very word museology, which is what this book is all about, although current in the profession for a generation or more, has not yet found its way into some of the more widely-used dictionaries.

It could be said that to some extent the fault lies with the museums. Their purpose and functions are subject to seemingly endless debate within the profession, and those dedicated to research have perhaps not yet fully come to terms with those who believe museums are teaching institutions, as will be seen in Chapter XI, 'The Present Dichotomy'. Indeed, as their needs grow, both sides become more demanding in terms of money, effort and space, and their differences are emphasized. The front which museums present to the world is therefore in some apparent disarray. A positive policy, singleness of purpose, are useful arguments in justifying one's case in a crisis-torn, disillusioned and hard-headed world, and museums are not able to put them forward.

Most museums are paid for out of the public purse. That they do give value for money spent on them I have no doubt, because I am well aware of the range of services which they offer, but I question if I could make out a case which on the face of it would

48

convince the average unsympathetic taxpayer in an inflationary era. However unwillingly, the ordinary man will accept spiralling expenditure on the health service, or on education, because their purposes are self-evident, but, even if they are linked to education, museums and galleries he looks upon as unnecessary. They spend his money. What he gets back from them in return is not obvious, unless he happens to be among the percentage of the population who make regular visits to them. In his eyes, in fact, they are unproductive, and so they are unproductive to most of those he is likely to vote for in local or central government elections, likewise to most of those who hope to sell their goods or services to the same ordinary man, or woman. We have to convince him or her, and those they vote into power, not only of what museums are doing already for the community, but of what they are poised to do and capable of doing. Because it is reasonable that everything which is paid for out of the public purse should directly or indirectly benefit the taxpayer or the ratepayer.

All institutions supported by such public funds should have a function which recognizably integrates them with the community. My definition of such a function would of course include the display of works of art for pure enjoyment by the public, because I happen to believe that enjoyment of the arts in one form or another is essential to the full well-being of a civilized community; but I also believe that relatively few people in our etiolated urban communities of today are capable of appreciating such works as they were meant to be appreciated, or of distinguishing between what is valid and what invalid in art, just as they have lost the power of distinguishing between nourishing and unnourishing foodstuffs, which leads us back to the educational function of museums. Such education is something much more important and exciting than the mere organizing of short courses on the history of Byzantine painting, or the Quattrocento, or Louis XV furniture. It is a question of trying to restore to the community that appetite for the aesthetic experience which is natural to man.

I have in front of me as I write a couple of agricultural implements made for use in a modern African community, both of them not only beautiful in form but also lightly decorated because the maker obviously delighted in what he was doing and

49

expected the owner to take pleasure in using them—both of them also, incidentally, more efficient for their purpose than their counterparts in my own toolshed. Here we are at the grass-roots of the aesthetic experience. I believe the man who made these implements would derive much more from a confrontation with, say, Michelangelo's Pietà in St Peter's than would almost any western factory worker. The factory worker has probably lost both his sense of wonder and his feeling for craftsmanship. Recovery of this simple delight in a supreme work of beauty is, to my mind, on a level with the conquest of pollution, but very nearly nothing is being done about it. Responsibility for such recovery must be laid upon some body, or bodies, which have access to a wide range of human artifacts, from the most primitive to the most sophisticated. The obvious body is the museum, which has the custody of more and more of our inheritance of beauty; but if the museum is to do what needs to be done it will have to be taken very seriously indeed, not only by the authorities who finance it but also by the curatorial staff.

The potential of museums in the social sense is more easily illustrated by reference to museums of science and technology than to museums of art. Science museums are later comers in the evolution of the movement and have less to live down. Not all of them have been able to get their inheritance from the Industrial Revolution into perspective, to master it and marry it to modern advances in technology, but the greater institutions are all alert to their duty of interpreting what is going on today to the widest possible public, and to such familiar institutions as the London Science Museum and the Deutsches Museum one might at random add the names of the Palais de la Découverte in Paris and, in the United States, the Chicago Museum of Science and Industry, the Franklin Institute of Philadelphia and the New York Museum of Science and Industry, and of course the new Smithsonian in Washington, so different from the old. The contribution of the American institutions was described as far back as 1939 by T. R. Adam in an essay in an interesting book called *The Museum and Popular Culture* (American Association for Adult Education, New York), and the points he made are more than ever applicable today. His theme is what would now be called the technological explosion. The social effects of scientific advance and the reaction of workers to them came to an

early climax with the Luddites, but the confrontation has continued ever since. Its repercussions overtax our politicians in
every session of Parliament because of resultant labour disputes,
and plague the community with accidents, pollution and social
evils of many sorts. That fear of the machine which society
thought preposterous in 1811 is today become justified. Misery
is truly being created where there should be happiness, and it is
happening under an oblivion induced by a popular gadgetry which
the machine itself makes possible, causing unrest with no obvious
cause, strikes which one suspects the strikers themselves do not
really understand.

We are not learning to live with the machine. As the machine
grows more sophisticated, the problem grows worse. Responsibility lies more and more with a few specialists who, by their
very training, are more often than not unfitted to make decisions
on the ethical questions their work gives rise to. Democracy
places responsibility upon the elected representatives of the
people, but neither people nor representatives have the knowledge to judge the significance of 'progress' and are at the
mercy of the specialists. This 'Doomwatch' situation is only too
familiar to us all. The solution is certainly not a neo-Luddite
smashing of atomic reactors nor a consumer strike against the
use of pollutants, even if those were possible. Hope seems to lie
in educating the public in the broad principles of the main lines
of scientific and technological advance so that it can form
reasoned judgements and influence its representatives accord-
ingly. In the nineteenth century this kind of popular education
was accomplished by the mechanics' institutes, later perhaps by
the workers' educational associations which played such a part in
shaping the outlook of Labour politicians in the early days of the
movement. Today, no one form of education can cope with the
task of keeping the public informed about what is happening in
science and technology. Adult education classes touch a relatively small part of the community: their appeal is much less
than when the hunger for knowledge sprang from a political
urge. Television does something to help. There is however
something essentially ephemeral about a medium in which one
topic perpetually drives out another from a screen a few inches
square. The museum, in its new concept, could make this area
of education its own.

To examine the problem a little more closely, some of our museums already explain the older forms of industrial processes fairly satisfactorily. For example, the application of steam power can be followed from the day of the beam-engine to the appearance of the supercharged locomotive. Things which cannot be exhibited by reason of their size—industrial plant, for example, or marine engines—are shown in the form of models. There is enough here to inform anyone of an inquiring mind on some of the main technical aspects of applied steam power. The economic and social aspects of the story of steam, however, tend to be ignored. Even the staggering impact of the Industrial Revolution is generally taken as understood. This of course is adding another dimension to the accepted scope of the technological museum, and it can be argued that such subjects should be covered by museums of local history such as the Museum of London, or the Museum of the City of New York, or Historiska Museet in Göteborg, which among other things deals with the effects of emigration. Contemporary technology in all its complexity is a challenge to the most courageous director. Here I am sure it is impossible for one museum to deal with everything, technical processes on the one hand and their effects upon society on the other. Industries are no longer assemblages of vast machines embodying simple processes easily demonstrated, but exhibit merely corridors of dials and computer banks, and the intricacy of what goes on behind the streamlined façade is nearly impossible to break down into the sort of museum display which will interest and instruct the layman. But this gulf of ignorance between production and the people needs to be bridged by some form of interpretation, and there is little doubt museums have the capability of doing it.

Or perhaps I should say they can do it if there is a large-scale involvement of industry itself. Already there is a close link between industry and most of the larger museums of technology, but we must aim for a stage when industrialists will recognize the service which museums can render as they already recognize the universities and technical colleges, endowing chairs and donating money for research. I appreciate that in making this plea it may be read with scant enthusiasm by some museum directors, because the flow of gifts from industry to certain institutions brings pressure on their space. I realize too that it is very easy for someone like myself, no longer with any responsibility in the matter, to recommend. I can only say that in museums of science and technology the need to plan rigidly and to accept only what is strictly relevant to the plan, at least for exhibition purposes, has to be observed, and that there must be storage in some area where space is less costly than in the city centres for anything which cannot make a significant contribution to current display. Adjustment between man and his environment is one of the main requisites of human happiness. Science and industry are creating a new and largely incomprehensible environment, and social unrest is a reflection of this, so they have a duty to support any institution which can help enable man to comprehend some at least of the more significant things which are happening to him. The dangers inherent in technocracy are far greater than those posed by past tyrannies, because a technocracy is more difficult to overthrow; but on the other hand if we can catch up with our technology we may recover some of the pleasure in it felt when Adam delved and Eve span.

Natural history museums should in the same way systematically interpret developments in the biological sciences. Pollution of our environment, for example, burst upon the awareness of the general public almost like a thunderclap, partly perhaps because it was made a feature of International Conversation Year. Pollution had been intensifying over generations, and the evidence was there for the looking. If our natural history museums had been less preoccupied with a new look for their old methods of display, more alert about conditions governing the survival of the fauna they were exhibiting, including *homo sapiens* himself, agitation aimed at halting what was happening might have begun earlier than it did.

Conservation of the world's natural resources, their redistribution, the potentialities of deposits of oil or natural gas, or of uranium and other new sources of power, the possible 'spin-off' benefits of space exploration: none of these are matters which either the public or administrations would normally associate with museums; yet where can the ordinary man turn who has neither the time nor capacity to consult the relevant publications, many of them technical, if he wants to keep himself informed about what is happening in fields which do very much affect him sooner or later? Where technology or geology are primarily

53

involved, as with nuclear power or metal deposits, he can glean a great deal of information in the appropriate museum. Glean, however, is perhaps the right word, and he will certainly be hard put to find in any museum I know displays which indicate the economic significance of new inventions or of new sources of power or wealth, or their likely impact upon the community. The only museum I know of which does seem to attempt to answer this sort of problem in some measure is the Philadelphia Commercial Museum, a vast complex of halls which house a bewildering variety of temporary exhibitions. It fulfils in the United States a rôle at one time described as giving it some of the functions of the Empire Marketing Board in Britain. The Commonwealth Institute in London has perhaps some points in common with the Philadelphia museum, as for example its elaborate services for school children. The American institution, which is run by the city, also covers town and country planning and by means of permanent working models illustrates proposed developments, not only in the city but in the whole Delaware valley. This is a good example of the intelligent use of a museum by a local authority and contrasts with the countless municipalities which regard their museums merely as dumping places for local by-gones.

Briefly to revert to the visual arts, surely museums should have the same sort of interpretative function in relation to contemporary trends as they so obviously have in the field of technology, although it would be difficult to find agreement about how this should be done. Already, in Chapter III, I have expressed my uneasiness about public institutions, occupying an authoritative, to some an even oracular position, setting the seal of their approval on contemporary work. Painting and sculpture have always been media for highly personal statements, but more and more in our time have been pervaded by an assertiveness devoid of response to the expressed needs of society, and nearly impossible to assess in terms of ultimate significance. Curators are as susceptible as anyone to the influence of critics and of the artists themselves. I feel that the exhibition of contemporary sculpture and painting is properly the responsibility of the academies and of private or commercial galleries.

It is a different matter with an art such as stained glass, and with the crafts and industrial art. This is work having some degree of integration with the community, and with some accepted standards of excellence by which it can be judged. Here the interpretative function of the museum may be exercised usefully. As to architecture and town planning and the whole question of amenity in the environment, I have already mentioned this is dealt with in the Philadelphia Commercial Museum; and I certainly believe that in this country municipalities should have in their own museums temporary exhibition halls where the planning departments could put the often excellent displays of photographs and models illustrating their intentions, or offering alternative schemes, which at present they sometimes place in shops or even derelict premises. Indeed, it might well be the museum rather than the planning authority which should devise such exhibitions, so that proposals could be projected with greater objectivity; and the museums might work hand-in-hand with bodies such as the Royal Fine Art Commission, whose task at present regrettably tends to be rather remote from the public. In the field of the artist-craftsman, from time to time in my capacity as a museum official I have collaborated with the Arts Council, the Craft Centres and with the Worshipful Company of Goldsmiths and have received the warmest support. There are many organizations, too, which are less well known, encouraging craftsmen sometimes in the remoter areas, and periodic critical reviews of their work by major museums with large public attendances would ensure wider recognition.

I wrote earlier that the fault in this matter of taking museums seriously to some extent lies with the museums. There is the divisive difference of views among staff about the conservational and educational functions; but there is also a certain built-in unwillingness among some academic staff to make what amount to positive assertions on controversial topics. I have encountered this attitude myself on more than one occasion, as when I suggested that an exhibition on the causes of pollution would be timely. Opposition was raised on two grounds: first, that such an exhibition might offend certain vested interests, and that this was inappropriate in a national institution, and second that reputations for scientific objectivity could be endangered. Both arguments had some substance. However, it is just because a national or any other large museum has a solid reputation that its exhibitions will carry weight, and if, after exhaustive sifting of the

55

evidence, its staff come to certain conclusions it should have the courage of its convictions. The alternative is to regard museums purely as encyclopaedias. This, virtually, would be to reduce them again to collections, which is something I have already said they are not. After all, I recall a dogged anti-Darwinian retired colonel roundly condemning in a letter to the press the evolution gallery in my own museum. Progress would be impossible without the drawing of conclusions. Unless they adopt a positive, even at times an assertive policy, museums cannot expect society to take them very seriously.

But museums cannot pull themselves out into the main stream of affairs entirely by their own efforts. Though the profession has many distinguished members, few of them find their way into the higher councils of the nation where they can press their case at the highest level, as lawyers, for example, or industrialists so often do. There has been too much tinkering with the question of museums and galleries, too many tedious little tugs-of-war about purchase grants, too few extended debates involving general principles such as took place in the Lords, particularly over admission charges. A major investigation is needed not merely on what museums are doing, but on what part they and other bodies and institutions linked to the educational system might play in interpreting great issues to the community. If it is necessary to multiply the number of universities and colleges and to alter their characters to produce candidates for top jobs in the modern world, then it is necessary to educate the electorate which pays for it all, and which has to take the consequences of right or wrong decisions made. Adult education, to quote T. R. Adam again, is 'an essential framework for political democracy'. The museum, as I see it, could be the best possible vehicle for promoting such adult education in many of its aspects. A systematic scrutiny of its possibilities by educationists and sociologists, as well as by industrialists, is long overdue, and a working party should be set up in which specialists in those fields can co-operate with members of the museum profession, perhaps through the Museums Association.

VI *The Problem of Presentation*

THE REVOLUTION in display methods which has taken place since the First World War is perhaps not fully realized by anyone except those few members of the museum profession who have survived this period. I have always had a particular interest in this problem, and my recollections of the changes must cover half a century. I remember halls of towering plaster-casts ranging from metopes from the Parthenon to Pisan pulpits and other technically remarkable gothic reproductions: and there were those close formations of model locomotives and steamships and, of course, also not so far off in time, the ethnographical congestions at the British Museum and elsewhere. Display, in those days, was a function of the academic staff, and their aim usually was to show as much as they could. The First World War was followed by a different outlook. Perhaps partly as a result of exhaustion and of a decrease in public purchasing power, in the twenties selectivity began to exercise a stronger appeal. It was reflected in shop-window displays, where milliners and others tended to show a few choice things where they had formerly crowded their shelves, and one could feel it strongly influencing some of the great international exhibitions such as the Paris Exposition of 1925 and the British Empire Exhibition at Wembley. Its influence spread to the museums in the thirties. Here again perhaps exhibitions took the lead, and the striking displays of Persian Art and Chinese Art at Burlington House, largely devised by museum men such as Sir Leigh Ashton, which to the plaudits of the critics emphasized the sheer beauty of isolated pieces— one remembers the impact of the great T'ang Lohan figure and of Hsia Kuei's painting, 'A Myriad Miles of the Yangtse'—so that the museums had no alternative but to begin to stress their chief treasures instead of leaving them to be discovered among lesser pieces. It signalled the beginning of the end of stuffiness.

My own personal reaction at this time is probably fairly typical

57

of the converted. Emphasis of the individual piece meant attempts to obliterate everything irrelevant. Some of us, for example, campaigned to eliminate the funereal black frames of the glass cases which we had inherited from Victorian times—in mourning, they used to tell us, for the death of the Prince Consort, who had in fact laid the foundation stone of my museum shortly before he died. Black paint was exchanged for pale tones to merge with the walls beyond. There was opposition to this innovation, but precedents were being set by some of the newer galleries such as the Whitworth at Manchester, and by the outbreak of war in 1939 some of the primary galleries in the big museums could boast a considerable elegance.

Professional display staffs of today may not see many virtues in the compromise era which immediately followed the war of 1939–45. It can, however, be contended that this era laid the foundations of the new attitude towards display. It certainly convinced some academic staff that the aesthetics of display were worth serious study; but more than this, in itself it achieved certain results which are being lost sight of. It was entirely an amateur affair: responsibility lay with academic staff who happened to have good taste and, in a few cases, an instinct for design. They might have said it was no part of their jobs to devise attractive displays, except that in those days there was no one else to do the work and there may have been a vague clause in their conditions of employment to the effect that they would be responsible for what went on show in the public galleries. Everything on the display side is now done much more knowledgeably and efficiently. Until as late as the sixties, nevertheless, there was a certain air, perhaps dilettante at times, but conveying conviction and personality—an air maybe of the home of a great and discerning collector—informing the best presentation in some of the national and the greater municipal art museums. I have not forgotten that elsewhere I have condemned the notion that the modern museum is an extension of the private collection of the past; but this is not to deny that the collector, like the direct patron, can be more than a mere purchaser and may help to link a work of art with the community at large by the very context in which he puts it, even adding minutely to its stature or charm by an implied comment, as Chinese collectors in fact have done by placing their stamps on masterpieces of painting

58

which came into their possession. The stamp of the collector who merely groups his possessions significantly is ephemeral. In museums the stamp of certain men may fade in a little while, but sometimes—Ashton's in the Victoria and Albert, for example—it may linger, and brash new assistant-keepers might well think twice before obliterating it completely. Nor will the lack of it be compensated by any amount of professional finish. I am not so sure, either, that the expertise of the professionals will, in the field of the temporary exhibition, ever quite replace the enthusiastic amateurism in display which inspired some of the best of the great international exhibitions of the twenty years or so which followed the war. There is, if nothing more, an individuality about the exhibition contrived by the keen academic specialist which can never quite be achieved by the trained man or woman who knows all the stock answers in the textbooks or in the repertoire of exhibition contractors.

The revolution which has brought in expert display staff in its latter stages has been a fairly rapid one, at least in Britain. As happens with revolutions, it has hurt many members of the *ancien régime*, probably none more than those men and women of taste who are now told to stick to their proper field of scholarship. Sometimes they have a case for resisting. The source of a great deal of the expertise needed for new methods of presentation must be the commercial world, and it is all too easy to forget that a museum display-case simply is not a shop-window. The basic philosophy of window-dressing is deception and seduction. The aim of museum display is pleasurable instruction. The training available to most potential museum display staff up to now has been such as will fit them for commercial display work, and it is hardly surprising if a high proportion of academic staff look upon the introduction of display staff as being contrary to the interests of the museum. It can be argued that the museum is out to 'sell' a commodity—visual education—to the public. It is not however a commodity in competition with other brands of the same thing, and the vulgarity which is such a prominent element in cut-throat commercial competition is not only out of place in a museum, but destroys the very things which the museum stands for.

It will be said there is a high-grade professional designer available to the museums in the display-consultant, who has been behind most of the successful public exhibitions of contemporary design and craftsmanship in recent years. He is in a very different category from the shop-window experts, and his achievements are often striking and memorable. One might cite as examples of his work some of the exhibitions mounted at Goldsmiths' Hall in London, and the craft pavilions in great international exhibitions and trade fairs. Indeed, the display-consultant has been used again and again by the museums themselves, notably for temporary displays. I think, however, it is fair to say that temporary should be the operative word, for as a rule there is an element of the elusive, the bizarre, and ultimately the ephemeral which, however charming in a temporary exhibition, is wholly inappropriate to a permanent gallery demanding regular return visits over a long period. There are also practical considerations. The attention to conservation which must be built into any permanent method of display in a museum is difficult to achieve by the means utilized in such temporary exhibitions. Thus few people except those who have some experience in museums have much idea of the dust problem which plagues all museums in cities, still less of the problems of atmospheric pollution, which are constantly multiplying. It is nearly impossible to exclude either dust or noxious gases from even the most solidly-constructed display-case, or vitrine as it is now commonly called, if there is to be access to the specimens it contains; and such access there must be in the most permanent display, not only because the condition of the objects has to be inspected periodically, but also because vibration caused by visitors and by traffic in the street outside causes them to 'creep'. Display-consultants mainly with experience of temporary exhibitions have little or no familiarity with such problems. It is rare to find a case designed by one of them which will fulfil the requirements of the permanent galleries. Things might be rather different if museums were totally air-conditioned; but air-conditioning is a vastly expensive undertaking. The need to work with one eye constantly on a very close budget is in general something to which the display-consultant is much less accustomed than is the administrative staff of a museum.

Having said these things, I will devote the remainder of this chapter to discussing display staff, because in fact their importance to the modern museum can hardly be over-estimated.

I might add that I introduced a display department in my own museum at a time when only two or three other national institutions in this country had done so.

Recruitment, as I have already indicated, is a very real problem. The intake of design staff to museums and galleries is infinitely small by comparison with the needs of industrial and commercial concerns, and therefore in training the bias is all towards commercial display. Not only is the psychology of commercial display quite different from that of museum display, but the attitude towards the 'goods' displayed must also be totally different. Commercial goods are expendable—indeed the ultimate aim is to get rid of them as quickly as possible—and the responsibility of display staff in handling them is not a great matter, whereas museum specimens as often as not are irreplaceable and careful handling of them is of the first importance. Not that I suggest candidates for museum display posts are particularly likely to be casual in their attitude to the material. One has to be equally vigilant with candidates for junior museum posts, who usually come straight from secondary school. But the young boy or girl who is attracted to museum life normally has a special interest in the things he finds in museums, whereas the candidate for a display post is, quite naturally, interested primarily in effects he may achieve. Display assistants are for the most part drawn from colleges of art. Respect for materials certainly should be basic to the disciplines taught in such colleges, but in recent years this seems to have had very low priority in some colleges at least, and indeed one might almost say that the contemporary approach to the arts has something very like a built-in contempt for materials and techniques and for the whole philosophy of *ars longa* which it is part of the purpose of art museums to inculcate. Obviously, therefore, in selecting the right man or woman to head the museum display staff one must look for much more than professional expertise. One must look for an attitude which is all too rare. One must look for someone who, although familiar with all the modern techniques, is yet on the side of the academic staff in his eagerness to bring out the significance of the things to be displayed. He must of course be able to attract to him assistants who are of a like mind.

Here it is as well to remember that 'of a like mind' does not mean imitation. A. E. Parr (*Mostly about Museums*, page 43) warns that 'no museum should be governed in its presentations by the taste and preferences of any single person'. The monotony which can result from the repetition even of excellence can, he maintains, be deadly in a large institution, and he pleads for the freedom of gifted individuals to express themselves. This is a warning to be heeded carefully. It is not unknown for a director, far less an exhibitions officer, to insist on having his way even with the details of a display. Elsewhere I have said that the director of a museum should have in him an element of the creative artist, but this does not mean that no one else on his staff should have the right to express himself in his own way. The exhibitions officer also must encourage creativity among his assistants.

One of the teething problems of introducing display staff, as most museum administrators have always expected, is to reconcile the exhibitions officer with the academic staff, who are naturally suspicious of the capability of anyone trained in a different sort of discipline to have any dealings with the material for which they have responsibility. This applies in museums of natural history and technology quite as much as in art museums. It is all too easy for serious tensions to develop between the new department and the old departments, and there may be years of difficulty and frustration for the exhibitions officer, who by the very fact that he is in some degree an artist may be more than usually sensitive to criticism. He must certainly be endowed with tact. The tact of the director of the museum himself will also be put to the test, and this especially in an institution of high academic repute, where the keepers and even some of the assistant-keepers are specialists internationally recognized, possessing almost complete autonomy in their area of the museum. The director is in the difficult position of having to weigh the interests of such members of his senior staff against the crying need to improve his public galleries. The one thing he must not do, even in the face of obduracy, is to go over the head of his academic staff. In judgements involving the safety or the significance of a specimen theirs, rather obviously, must be the last word.

Yet however carefully handled the process of introducing display staff may be, sooner or later the public galleries, or some of them, are likely to become a sort of disputed territory. It will be essential to find a compromise between the two extremes, equally unthinkable, of barring exhibition staff from a gallery or of handing over the gallery to them to do as they like with the contents. It is perfectly true that some members of academic staffs are totally incapable of selecting what is significant to the casual visitor because they cannot see the wood for the trees. It is equally true that an exhibitions officer, even of considerable experience, cannot be expected to know which things, *sui generis*, are significant in a collection which is unedited. The problem is purely one of human weaknesses and personalities. The solution is probably best reached through a series of meetings in which both sides are well primed with the other's point-of-view and everybody is ready to be reasonable. If that seems to be a counsel of perfection, there is plenty of evidence that it can be made to work. If the academic staff will prepare a blueprint of their aims and list the means at their disposal to achieve them, it is for the exhibitions officer to put forward a layout which the academic staff will scrutinize and criticize before the whole thing goes forward to the stage of a model and working drawings. No doubt there are as many ways of managing this exercise in co-operation as there are museum directors. The important thing to establish early is mutual respect between the two sides. They must realize that the public galleries are not in fact disputed territory, but common ground where two sorts of knowledge are married to create a new public image for museums.

As I have already said in Chapter IV, the exhibitions officer and display staff have a critical rôle to play as interpreters between the academic staff and architect. However, it is in his capacity to bring professional standards to the presentation of the museum collections that the exhibition officer's chief importance lies. Earlier in this chapter I may seem rather to have eroded this importance by dwelling on the virtues of the efforts of academic staff in the public galleries, some of which had distinguished results. But it would be absurd to contend that even the most talented curator could ever compete in this area with the best professionals, whose knowledge of methods and materials, allied to taste and imagination, can penetrate to new dimensions in museum display. I have heard one or two of my colleagues say they considered exhibition officers' appointments should be for limited periods. Their argument is that, confined

63

in one museum, they will become in-grown and their creative powers will be blunted, or perhaps etiolated is the word. This could of course apply in a very small museum. In a large one I am sure there is little such danger, as the challenges are constant and varied and the area so great that no man could cover it in his lifetime. Nevertheless, it is important that all display staff should have frequent opportunities for seeing what is going on in the world outside, not merely in other museums and galleries but in other fields of exhibition designing; and it is equally important that they should be kept in touch with new developments in the disciplines covered by the museum, for it is part of an alert exhibition officer's job to sense opportunities, perhaps before academic staff realize they exist. The exhibition officer, as a museum man, has a big advantage over the outside design consultant in this respect.

For the right type of exhibition officer the challenge of the museum is an enthralling one. I think if I had my time over again this might be the side of museum work that I would choose. I have already argued that the museum is not a collection, nor yet a building. It is an idea, or complex of ideas, and what more splendid task can any imaginative designer ask for than to materialize ideas by grouping or projecting supreme examples of the creative powers of nature and of man? Demands upon him may range from a simple exercise of taste such as forming a setting for an arrangement of Sung pottery or an almost clinical display of perfect gemstones to the gigantic possibilities offered by such subjects as the ecology of vanishing species, the exploration of outer space, or the attempt to present a valid commentary on races which have left little behind them but dumb monumental evidence, such as the Aztecs or the Picts. A stage-designer may derive huge satisfaction from attempting to match his talents to the genius of a great playwright. Museum display work of the future could be every bit as rewarding, with the difference that the artist must conceive on a basis not of fancies but of facts, in so far as those are known.

Yet even the theatrical mood is not ruled out. It may well be justified, for instance, in a temporary exhibition aimed at leaving a dramatic impression of the scope of some man of genius. It was inevitable in the Berlioz exhibition at the Victoria and Albert Museum, as in the Diaghilev exhibition mounted for the first

Edinburgh International Festival in 1947. All the time new dimensions of presentation add to the possibilities. New methods of lighting, new materials, new electronic devices bring revolutionary effects within the designer's grasp. Visual effects may be increased by aural ones. Considerable advances have been made in sound commentaries, both portable and static, which often can replace printed labels; but perhaps more interesting from the angle of the exhibition officer is the use of tape-recording devices in, for example, exhibits of song-birds. Such tapes may be used even for background sounds to suggest atmosphere, particularly in temporary exhibitions, and one recalls the not-unsuccessful attempt to indicate the presence of carrion crows which carried the imagination one stage further with the reconstruction of the sinister Roquepertuse temple in the Royal Scottish Museum's version of the exhibition of Early Celtic Art in 1970. There is really no reason why any of the five senses should have nothing to offer in museum display.

VII *The Case for a Comprehensive Museum*

By A COMPREHENSIVE museum is meant a general museum, covering several disciplines. At one time far more museums were comprehensive than were otherwise. Under their roofs could be found anything from paintings and plaster-casts to stuffed animals and superannuated machinery. More than any other sort of museum, they typify the bad old tradition, the tradition of an institution serving as a dump for things for which the community has no further use: or alternatively, the tradition of the museum as the hobby of a crank with magpie proclivities. Metropolitan members of the museum profession probably tend to regard the comprehensive museum as something of an anachronism, and some of the larger museums which are still comprehensive have subdivided themselves into more or less rigid departments regarding their sister departments virtually as other museums. This trend is emphasized by the modern practice in certain large museums of recruiting staff who are already specialists, or who have been shaped as specialists at university. The man or woman whose interests are general and not particular may find it difficult to get a senior job in the larger museums today.

No doubt I am prejudiced on this matter. For some years I directed what is possibly the largest comprehensive museum in this country, and therefore have come to think and plan in terms of the comprehensive museum. However, allowing for prejudice, I still believe there is a strong case for not abandoning too readily the comprehensive tradition. I say this partly because I agree with those who believe there are grave dangers in the educational swing towards greater and greater specialization, the swing commonly described as knowing more and more about less and less. This seems inevitable under what I have referred to earlier as a technocracy. Attention to detail may make possible journeys to the moon, but the minute analyses on which so much 'progress' depends puts blinkers on considerable sections of the population, and constant effort is needed to make them aware of the world as

66

a whole and to educate them in the relationships on which balanced living depends. Even the climate which breeds industrial troubles is fostered by basic ignorance of what the other man does and what his problems are. So that if we accept the usefulness of museums in the system of education we must, I think, accept that there is a strong case for the comprehensive museum, both small and large. By saying this I am not of course hinting that it would be a good thing for all museums to 'go comprehensive', and that the British Museum, Bloomsbury, should again join forces with the British Museum, South Kensington. I am merely warning against the kind of thinking which is based on the inevitability of existing comprehensive museums eventually splitting up into groups of smaller, specialist museums. Some exciting possibilities would be lost if this ever came about.

I base the case for developing the comprehensive idea on circumstances ruling in what was my own museum, because similar circumstances apply in other large institutions of the kind. The museum in question embraces four departments: Art and Archaeology, omitting European painting but including ethnography; Natural History; Geology and Mineralogy; and Technology. Divisions between departments traditionally were hard and fast, with no particular bonds of sympathy or outlook between departmental staffs. The first project to bring about major inter-departmental co-operation was the decision to have an introductory hall of biology, designed to trace the appearance and evolution of life on the earth. Clearly all the earlier evidence, the fossil evidence, fell within the province of the Department of Geology, which covers palaeontology. The later material had to be drawn from the Department of Natural History. There could be no firm line of demarcation between the two. A small team was selected, drawn from the academic staff of the two departments, and this team continued to guide progress throughout, negotiating with exhibition staff and with the architects and engineers of the Department of the Environment, which has responsibility for all such constructional work in the national museums. There were of course many differences of opinion, especially in the earlier stages, and there were resignations from the team, but it proved an effective controlling body over the necessary period of several years of planning and building, and it was small enough to maintain fixity of purpose, enthusiasm and momentum.

The philosophy underlying the comprehensive museum, and which did in fact have a part in forming early museums, is the rather pompous-sounding one that a museum should reflect all creation: the creative activities, that is, both of nature and of man. There is therefore a logical continuity, not only from the laying down of the earth's rocks right through to the exploration of space, but embracing any side-issues on the way which may seem to help complete the picture. One of the problems in my museum has been the existence of a large hall just within the main entrance, a very lofty hall surrounded by galleries, the construction of which resembles that of the old Crystal Palace and dates from only a few years later than that centrepiece of the Great Exhibition. As a perfect example of this type of architecture, by general consent the hall was sacrosanct and changes in the fabric were forbidden. Since it was quite unsuited to normal museum displays, dwarfing all but gigantic objects and at the same time admitting so much light that many types of object must deteriorate if displayed there, from our point-of-view this hall seemed very much of a white elephant. Although in itself a sort of exhibit, as a place to house exhibits it was a liability, or apparently so. One function it did seem capable of performing, however, was as an introductory hall to the entire museum; it seemed to have potentialities as the site for a symbolic display illustrating the one-ness of creation as well as its infinitude. This no-man's-land could become an area for establishing by means of a few bold exhibits the concept of the Whole Man, and I was inclined to call it the Hall of Leonardo. What I am elaborating now is a scheme that was when I left the museum still little more than a thought in my mind, a scheme which had not even reached the stage of a preliminary sketch, so there is no particular likelihood it will ever materialize; and as it is the sort of scheme which reflects my contention that directing a museum should involve a measure of creative artistry, my concept of what might be would be far different from another's.

I envisaged groupings of massive objects, each significant of a particular area of the museum's field. Size seemed important for two reasons: first because an immense floor and spatial volume had to be filled, second because dramatic impact upon a visitor entering the hall was essential. Among objects of a kind suitable for display were a large specimen of fossil-bearing rock, the skeleton of a dinosaur, perhaps the reproduction of an area of cave-painting from Lascaux or Altamira, a *mihrab* from India, a totem-pole from British Columbia, a Greek column, a windmill, a large example of steam-driven machinery, a great clock, a state coach, a glider, a spacecraft. It is a random list. Selection would depend upon how meaningful an object might be in the context of the hall. Thus the clock, as Mumford elaborately demonstrates, is the very mainspring of so many mechanical inventions, and the wheel too is a vast step forward in man's material progress. Cave-paintings, or alternatively Bushman drawings from the Kalahari or rock-carvings from the Bohuslan district of Sweden, illustrate the birth of art from primitive belief in magical powers. The state coach is a social status symbol as well as a means of transport, and has a sort of trumpet quality in a big confined space, as anyone entering the great hall of Nordiska Museet in Stockholm must agree. The glider, rather than an aeroplane, represents the basic principle of the heavier-than-air machine. As some of those things could be suspended in space, the problem hall would cease to be a monumental vacuum, and at the same time it would be made to function in a way which the generation which built it would have approved.

Co-operation between geologists and biologists is, of course, in no way remarkable. Some of the great natural history museums such as South Kensington and the American Museum in New York include departments of geology. Co-operation between art departments and either natural history or technology is quite another matter, as the disciplines involved are so totally different in their approach to their subjects, and although there are many scientists who appreciate art in one form or another, I would say there are far fewer art historians who, like the late W. B. Honey, show interest in the link between the sciences and the arts. To demonstrate that the two are merely different facets of one creation seems to me to be quite an important part of the educational process.

It is the will to demonstrate this, not the means, which is lacking. It is hardly necessary to point out that the arts are entirely indebted to technology for the tools and materials required. From the humblest craft levels to the most ambitious works of imagination those tools and materials dictate art forms and styles. The hard rock used by the Maya would never have lent itself to the requirements of the classical world, which could impose its intellectual concepts on the limestones and marbles so abundantly at its command. The subtleties of colour and texture which made the Chinese unrivalled masters of the ceramic arts derived from centuries of preoccupation with technical processes, culminating in the supremacy of the imperial porcelain-makers of Ching-te-Chen. The monk Theophilus and those of his like to whom we are indebted for the glories of the medieval cathedral were as much interested in the chemistry of what they did as in the spiritual message this made possible, as a glance at the *Diversarum Artium Schedula* shows. Indeed it might be said it is only when the arts come adrift from the craftsman's practical know-how, as in many ways they are doing today, that they are in danger of failing to justify themselves.

Whether one agrees with such conclusions or not, the marriage of art and technology is a fact, but it is not the sort of fact which art galleries underline, and thereby they lose an opportunity to re-establish that down-to-earth popular appeal which undoubtedly existed when the booths of potters and carvers and goldsmiths were familiar sights. Rarely in museum displays even of an art such as ceramics, so completely influenced by materials and processes, is there any attempt to demonstrate the *inevitability* of styles, given such factors as the wheel and certain clays, the local deposits of minerals, maximum temperatures in the available kilns; and the technologist may be so much better able to demonstrate such things effectively than the man whose studies have been directed mainly to the end-products. Surely it is obvious that the comprehensive museum, where technologists work under the same roof as ceramics specialists, in this respect could have certain advantages over a museum solely devoted to the arts? Certain great art museums do of course employ scientists in their laboratories, but they are research workers whose main job is to improve methods of identification and preservation. My point is that technical means and artistic end are inseparable, and that it is good that the museum should demonstrate this. Art does not just happen because a genius arises, or even because a measure of talent exists in a community, but is as much the inevitable product of natural resources and acquired skills as are the plough or the motor car.

Natural resources are the province of natural history museums and departments. In this age of specialization it does not seem odd that we should have to study the nature and distribution of metalliferous deposits in one institution, the techniques of working them in another, and in a third the manner in which they have been used for aesthetic ends. It is true that some modern archaeological museums have begun to tackle the enthralling job of showing how, for example, natural circumstances may shape civilizations. One can see very clearly in the Römisch-Germanisches Zentralmuseum in Mainz, or indeed in the Prehistoric and Romano-British Department of the British Museum as now laid out, how the Celts rose to power partly at least on the strength of the iron deposits of Central Europe, and by cultivating their resultant skills in metallurgy and metalworking dominated Europe long enough eventually to contribute an important element to what is now called Western culture. Archaeology is itself a comprehensive discipline. It is in treating of ages where the evidence does not have to be dug up that culture tends to come unstuck from its background, and the untutored might be forgiven for thinking the Renaissance was a purely artistic phenomenon if he learned about it only from museums. A big comprehensive museum which made full use of its resources could mount a Renaissance display of the most exciting kind.

There are of course comprehensive museums which have simply happened, and museums which have in a sense been deliberately created as comprehensive. It might be said the idea behind the Musée de l'Homme in Paris is comprehensive. Man in all his manifestations is as comprehensive a theme as one could demand, if it is extended to include the natural background to his activities. Until museums of this kind arose, anthropology and ethnography were too often represented by galleries which looked like junk-yards. Ethnography in particular had become something of an embarrassment, and was still so when I entered the museum service in the early thirties. In the pioneering days of the Empire, explorers, missionaries, soldiers and others sent back to Britain consignments of 'native' material which accumulated in the darker corridors of our museums, and even filled small local museums in towns where retired men and women from the outposts had tended to congregate. This material seemed to belong properly neither with art, archaeology, technology or natural history, and for generations attracted little academic interest and even less popular attention. In the course of time there were attempts to classify it. There was, for instance, the 'comparative' method, perhaps first practised, in this country at least, at the Horniman Museum in South London, and there was also the work of collectors like General Pitt-Rivers, who fully realized the value of such material in the study of anthropology, itself until comparatively recent times not properly recognized as a science, far less accepted as a university discipline. Recognition of the aesthetic qualities of many objects in this field by prominent painters and sculptors of the late nineteenth century and after gave ethnography a new sort of importance. Such pieces as Maori carvings and Benin bronzes and Yoruba masks attained high status and began to make record prices in the art market, and the cult of primitive art flourished, and still does. In some museums the art angle banished all other approaches to the subject. But in fact those big collections of ethnographical material, assembled just before the disintegration of the cultures which produced them, remain one of the great strengths of some of our comprehensive museums, with their lesson of the close relations between all man's activities.

For anyone for whom the world and all that is in it are an enduring enthralment, and who is determined that others must share his feelings, direction of a comprehensive museum must have a special appeal. I have heard it compared with being the conductor of an orchestra. There is a score to be interpreted, there are skilled instrumentalists in variety to be led, and there is an audience to captivate. The comparison could be made with the direction of any large museum, especially perhaps an art museum, but the effect attainable is more limited. My interpretation of the scope of the comprehensive museum may seem too grandiose for the more scholarly aspirant to a top post in the museum world, but it is simply not the job for a rigid specialist devoted to a single discipline. The director of an art or of a scientific museum can remain an art historian or a scientist and still administer his charge with success, but the director of a comprehensive museum for the time being at least must be a museum director and nothing else.

The proportion of what might be called 'floating vote' visitors is much higher in a comprehensive than in a specialist museum: visitors, that is, of no particular persuasion, or who have just 'come in out of the rain'. There are museum directors who have no use for this class of visitor. To my mind the casual visitor is a very important sort of visitor indeed, and the comprehensive museum is in a favoured position to do missionary work on behalf of museums as a whole, since potentially it has something for everyone. In its introductory halls and galleries it must assume only minimal knowledge in its visitors, whereas the specialist museum can go on the assumption that they have at least some idea of what they have come to see. There must be special emphasis on the introductory halls in any comprehensive museum. The indifference factor is so much higher here that some degree of attack is essential. The casual visitor, unlike the purposeful visitor in a specialist museum, has to be 'switched on' or he will leave as soon as he thinks the rain has stopped, leaving no impression in his mind. His attitude has to be converted, and very rapidly so, from a negative to a positive, receptive one. I believe the first step is to make him welcome, in the sense of making it pleasurable and encouraging for him to find himself where he is; and in a comprehensive museum one may do this without challenging his knowledge of or even his interest in any particular field. Thus it could be a mistake almost on the door-step to confront him with an elephant or a large bronze Buddha or a steam-engine, as any of these could be a misleading symbol of what lay beyond. Better to receive him in a pleasant but un-committed area such as the Garden Court in the Washington National Gallery, for all its somewhat Victorian conservatory atmosphere, and thence to an area where it can be made clear to him what the museum is all about, and where he can find keys to all the services offered.

Ancillary services possibly play a more vital part in a comprehensive than in any other sort of museum. As a rule it cannot compete with the specialist museum in the matter of publications, as it is much less rich in specific classes of material; but there is room for a whole literature of co-ordination relating one discipline to another, and there is room, too, for far more intro-ductory booklets aimed at the casual visitor. In the first category might be included such subjects as industrial art, amenity in town and country, conservation of both natural and artificial products. The lecture theatre in the comprehensive museum is perhaps in a position to achieve more popular success than lecture theatres in other museums, because it is possible to build up an intelligent regular audience from members of the community who like to hear authoritative comment on a wide variety of subjects. By drawing occasionally on distinguished chairmen, say from a neighbouring university or from industry, and on men and women of similar status to render votes of thanks and stimulate discussion, the museum platform can, as I know from my own experience, acquire something of the influence of such a body as the Royal Society of Arts, which interprets the word 'arts' much as I interpret the word comprehensive. The same promise of variety of programme gives the cinema in such a museum a wide appeal. So, too, with extra-mural activities, like the expeditions which are so popular with some American museums, ranging from local wildlife to country house art collections and tours abroad. Even here the comprehensive idea can increase popularity. I have particularly in mind the summer expeditions organized for the society of Friends of my own museum. Each of these might cover, say, an archaeological site or an historic mansion and also a nature reserve or perhaps an ancient mill. It is true the membership of such a society tends to be heavily biased on the side of the arts, as financial contributions to art purchases is normally one of the functions of these societies in general; but the response of all members to the offer of such mixed programmes is one of the rewards of having responsibility in a comprehensive museum.

VIII *Museums as a Profession*

RECRUITMENT TO MUSEUMS to some extent suffers from the popular image. Not that there is a lack of applicants for vacancies for most types of museum post, but in certain categories the proportion of suitable people is exceptionally low. Among the general public, which includes school leavers, there is an impression that people who like collecting things and browsing over them are obvious candidates for any kind of museum post, and among undergraduates of a certain sort there is a feeling that after some years of subsidized research at university it would be nice to end up in a museum and do research for the rest of one's life. It is unlikely that anyone thinking along those lines will fit in with the needs of a modern museum.

In fact, the museum of today, and perhaps still more the museum of the future, needs people who have a positive attitude to life, and can use men and women with a wide range of skills and inclinations, with the exception of those who are out to make a lot of money for themselves. Museums can use business men as well as scholars, organizers as well as artists, pushers as well as dedicated backroom-boys, but they cannot afford to recruit people whose main idea is to opt out of the wider world. This must be obvious to anyone who has read the preceding chapters, but it cannot be over-emphasized for those considering entering the museum profession. Every year museums become more complex and highly-organized, and there is less and less room for the eccentric devoted to a subject which matters to no one but himself. I say this with some faint regret because, like most people who have spent a lifetime in museums, I can remember some very endearing and amusing eccentrics who had somehow attached themselves to the place and become part of it, and so I hope there will always be corners in which the perpetual student can find refuge; but today the museum is financed by public funds and has a job to do, and it needs as shrewd and skilled staff as any other comparable establishment.

First, let us consider academic staff: not because in the future they will necessarily be more important than other categories, but because traditionally they are the determiners of the museum's character, and the pace-setters. In Great Britain in most of the larger museums they have been drawn straight from the universities with the qualification of a good honours degree. This degree was not always in a subject particularly relevant to the post where art museums are concerned, because the university has been regarded as the promoter of academic discipline rather than a training ground, the museum itself shaping recruits for its needs. As specialization has increased in the universities there has been more recruitment of people already knowledgeable in the field they are required for in the museum, and from time to time there is even some earmarking of candidates before they have taken their degrees. This was always possible on the scientific side. On the arts side it has become more possible since the universities instituted degree courses in such relevant subjects as archaeology, anthropology and the history of art. Now of course it is possible to specialize in art history and appreciation both at graduate and post-graduate level, and institutes like the Courtauld or the Warburg, or at Birmingham the Barber, offer training and research opportunities of international repute. What no university course on the arts side really is able to inculcate, however, is the knowledge which comes only through familiarity with actual art objects in quantity. Laurence Vail Coleman drew attention to this more than thirty years ago in the United States, and he extended the criticism to science courses. On interview boards on which I have served it has sometimes been the practice to introduce museum specimens as talking-points and tests, and I have seen a candidate with excellent academic qualifications confounded completely when confronted with something which he could have written a competent essay on once it was identified for him. It is not that one would expect a tricky identification from such a candidate. It is simply a question of the incapacity of some people ever to develop a 'feel' for things, and to marry this to academic knowledge. Without such a faculty a man or woman is of little use in a museum.

The best method of training is a *Kunstförscher* procedure, by which suitable people quite early in their university course are given the chance to opt for museum work and thereafter do what might be called their 'practical work' in the museums and galleries. The old objection to such early specialization was, quite rightly, that the intake to museums was too small to justify putting all one's eggs into one basket; but there has been a substantial increase in the number of opportunities for graduates in museums up and down the country, with even relatively small museums insisting on candidates possessing either a degree or the diploma of the Museums Association. As an added encouragement it should be remembered that the first-class art dealers require a very similar type of candidate, although his subsequent career will have a quite different slant. Such bracketing of museum and art market 'apprentices' is, I think, in line with the *Kunstförscher* tradition in Germany. To follow a similar practice with the scientific disciplines may seem less necessary, as students must of necessity spend much time handling specimens in the laboratory; but, as Coleman says, this is to give a broad knowledge of structure, function and behaviour and a grasp of research methods rather than acquaintance with the wide range and scope of great collections.

What has to be remembered more and more, however, is that the museum outlook is not as it used to be. In the first chapter I gave a passing warning about the 'collector' candidate, the man with a mania for collecting as such. It is right here to emphasize that sound academic accomplishment is quite as important as flair since, whether in science or in the arts, the museum professional must keep pace with the broad front of progress in his own and kindred fields and cannot afford to bury his head in his material. Weight of material can quite easily turn a man into the kind of ostrich referred to at the beginning of this chapter. In candidates, therefore, one should beware of what Coleman calls 'the low pressure individual': 'the man or woman seeking an easy way of life, protected from too keen competition'. The fact that museums are not usually asked to submit profit-and-loss accounts does not mean they can afford to carry passengers. I am repeating here what is said in the first two paragraphs, but doing so deliberately, because the caveat given there applies mainly to academic staff.

In the United States training specifically for the museum service has been available for something like half a century. Transatlantic universities, led by Harvard and Yale, which

77

possess first-class museums of their own, have trained many distinguished curators, and facilities have multiplied in recent years, although even there it should be said that academic training is dominant: training for art museums has a long lead over training for other sorts of museum and is very much a course in the history of art with the aim of producing curators. In this country, apart from Leicester and Manchester, I know of no university or college which offers a course of instruction in museum administration and curatorship. Such training is however offered through the Museums Association. It has taken a long time to build up a course of a weight and standard acceptable in terms of what a university might be expected to provide, but it is now widely recognized that the Diploma of the Associaciation is on the level of a degree. The problem with any such course is that it must be dual, that it must cover what Lawrence Vail Coleman calls 'learning and method'. The senior museum worker has to be knowledgeable not only in an academic discipline but in museum practice. The Museums Association course seeks to meet both requirements. The final examination comprises papers in a chosen discipline and also in museum method and practice. Its introduction already has raised the general level of competence in museum management far above that of a few years ago. However, it is never likely to replace the university. For higher museum posts the university will always be a prerequisite which the *ad hoc* course, however competent, cannot provide; yet equally no degree of inspired amateurism on top of academic distinction will obviate the need for mastery of museum method, so that university must be followed by some form of vocational training if the museum profession is to be worthy of the name.

The educational side of museum work undoubtedly will absorb an increasing number of staff. It is probable that this staff will include many qualified teachers, since the more museums co-operate with secondary schools the more essential it is that museum teaching staff are fully acceptable. But to lay down too rigid requirements for such posts would be a mistake. Most museum administrators come across people who have special gifts for conveying the meaning and significance of museum objects to others, both children and adults. Such gifts have nothing to do with certificates; and while the same sort of thing happens no doubt in schools, it is of special importance that museums should not miss opportunities of gaining such recruits. No educational aids, whether conventional labels or more sophisticated devices, will ever compensate for the lack of the man or woman with the capacity sympathetically to interpret the collections either to small groups in the galleries or in the lecture room, and especially to incapacitated children in desperate need of therapy of this kind.

There is a feeling in some quarters that any diversion of teachers from schools is unacceptable, but the numbers would be so small as to be derisory as an argument against, and it is probable the work would attract some for whom school teaching would have little appeal. In any event, museum teaching is totally different from school teaching. The work is identified with no particular class or school, but with a succession of schools and classes, and some may feel this sort of teaching must be remote and impersonal. Certainly there is little opportunity for the teacher to be able to watch and aid the progress of particular pupils over a period of years in the sense of shaping them as men and women; but the museum teacher might well be able to discern the leanings of individual pupils and to encourage them. Broadly, however, the museum teacher must identify with the collections he is interpreting rather than with pupils. And as to pupils, in most museums he may well be instructing adults as well as children.

Inevitably, too, administration will absorb some of the time, in certain cases the whole of the time of educational staff, as school requirements will always have to be reconciled with what the museum has to offer, and complex time-tables and transport problems must become more and more of a preoccupation, as any head of education services in a transatlantic museum will confirm. Another activity is the organization of special lectures, particularly 'celebrity lectures' for the general public, with the general aim of making the museum a platform for authoritative commentary and identifying it with leading thinkers. Every major museum needs one person at least to take the responsibility of administering such lectures, and such a duty calls for someone not only equipped with a liberal knowledge of who is who, but with the capacity and determination to get what he or she wants in the face of a great deal of frustration. This is a far

79

cry from the ability to evoke a response from elementary school children, but it is all part of the education service.

There are many professions within the museum profession. I refer particularly to those peculiar to museums, which present many problems both in recruitment and in training. One thinks, naturally, of the specialist technicians: the taxidermists and preparers in natural history museums, the restorers and craftsmen in art museums, the engineers and model-makers in technological museums. Each of those categories has its special problems, which it is not possible to discuss in a general book such as this, but some of those problems are of general interest. For instance, the skills which have to be developed, with accompanying responsibilities, are of a very high order, and although financial rewards are vastly improved in recent years, there is no doubt at all that in some cases at least some skills offered outside the museum profession would attract far higher pay. The precision and dedication demanded for the making and mounting of technological and scientific exhibits might well be more amply rewarded in industry, in pay-packets if not perhaps in satisfactions gained. Art restorers of long experience could command high fees if they linked themselves to the needs of the booming art market. As to the taxidermists, the fact that they have survived at all is probably mainly due to museums, as the few commercial concerns which took on apprentices have dwindled since the passing of the wealthy big-game hunter and the coming of preservation-orders on vanishing species of wild life. At the same time the meaning and scope of what used to be called taxidermy has altered out of recognition, and what at one time was a craft has become also a considerable art and at the same time a science, demanding knowledge of physics and chemistry, close familiarity with the habits, habitats and behaviour of animals, and a great deal of inborn taste, including a capacity to reconcile traditional realism with trends such as stylization of environment.

As to training for these professions within the profession, more and more this is controlled by the museums themselves. They train taxidermists for one another, including their colleague institutions overseas. For the art workshops and studios, they frequently recruit trainees from art colleges, but the real training of those only begins when they are faced with problems ranging from the disintegration of fabrics from a Peruvian burial site to the re-laying of an English satinwood veneer. There are invaluable manuals about basic principles such as H. J. Plenderleith's great work, *The Conservation of Antiquities and Works of Art,* but trainees are largely dependent upon their senior colleagues. A similar sort of challenge faces the recruit to the engineering workshop. No doubt he has served his time in some outside shop, but in the museum sooner or later he will find himself involved in situations completely strange to him—making a dilapidated phonograph look like new, perhaps, or assisting in re-rigging a modern fighter-plane. Model-makers have largely departed from museums, as it is much more economical to buy the models from commercial firms or from private sources; but I think technologists would agree that the making of precision scale models is a rare discipline for an apprentice, and the decline of the craft is a matter for much regret. Indeed, in these mini-professions the museums, almost without realizing it, are preserving traditions and attitudes to work once safeguarded by the medieval trade-guilds; and it is my feeling there will always be men and women who will opt out of the boredom of the modern industrial scene even if financially it does not pay them too well to do so.

Enough has been said about recruitment of display staff in the chapter on presentation. Here I might add that training—and it should be remembered that so far as the United Kingdom is concerned professional museum display is only a few years old— already is beginning to follow the lines of training sketched in the last paragraph. In brief, museums are setting their own standards and imposing their own methods, for the good reason that conditions differ widely from those prevailing in the commercial world. Here again, too, one must say that financial rewards outside may be greater than those obtainable in museums; but equally it must be emphasized that there is already a growing professional pride in jobs which are not quite like any comparable jobs outside. The early tendency to strained relations with other museum staff which existed in some places is unlikely to survive for many years, for the contribution of display staff to the museum's reputation is becoming obvious to all except the most hidebound academic.

One section of museum staff which has always tended to stand apart, in this country at least, is the clerical and administrative officers. This is a matter which affects large museums in the main, national or municipal. In the national museums such staff is usually drawn from a parent Civil Service department, and there may be much coming and going, as there is throughout the Civil Service, ultimate promotion in certain cases being attainable only by leaving the museum. In municipal museums, likewise, office posts of this kind are normally recruited from local government offices. Not infrequently the result may be a certain division of loyalties. Such officials quite naturally tend to look at museum problems through the eyes of their department and may well be critical of the real interests of the museum. From the point of view of the controlling department this is a good thing. There may even be certain benefits for the museum, which can gain substantial advantages from an officer's inside knowledge of administrative practice in the controlling department, thereby saving time and perhaps wasted effort. By and large, however, the dichotomy between museum and office staff is unfortunate. As museums become less and less ivory towers and more and more involved in the affairs of the community, their responsibilities grow heavier and their administration more complex, so they need all the momentum which complete solidarity of staff can give if they are to make full impact, and even a small sense of divided loyalties in key positions can erode this solidarity. The promotion problem may always be a barrier to the complete integration of administrative and professional staff, because in the foreseeable future few museums will be able to justify many high-level clerical posts. On the other hand, one does meet executive officers willing to sacrifice in some degree at least their promotion prospects just because they happen to like working in museums. Some compromise seems to be called for whereby the sacrifice may be minimized to enable the museum to benefit by the permanent service of such people.

Hitherto in Britain the new recruit has tended to join a particular museum rather than the museum profession, and often he stayed there for his entire career. For long enough there has been interchange between the staffs of provincial museums, and at directorial level even the national museums have seen such interchange, so that there is certainly much more fluidity than there used to be. Yet the national museums remain an exclusive sector of the profession. This is partly because national museum staff are Civil Servants, or virtually so in the case of national museums run by trustees. This exclusiveness is not a healthy thing. National museums in this country have many advantages which render their staffs something of an élite, this in spite of the fact that other museums, more especially the larger municipal and the university museums, possess specialist staff often every bit as competent as their counterparts in the national institutions. Readier interchangeability of posts would make a big difference in the museum profession. It might be added that even between the national museums there is relatively little interchange, though in theory such interchange should be simple enough. A man becomes identified with the collection over which he presides, and as he adds to it and spends years of research on it the collection becomes something like his own, and he would need greater inducements than can usually be offered to exchange it for another. Here we come back to the 'collection' mentality. Where museological interest is paramount, the museum man or woman is less reluctant to move on. The museum service will not attain its full potential until it has become less rigidly compartmentalized.

Coleman devotes considerable space to discussion of whether the museum profession is indeed a profession at all, although he himself has no doubts about it. He outlines the argument against, largely based on the variety of services and disciplines within the museum, which earlier writers contrasted with accepted professions such as medicine, the law and architecture. I do not think the museum profession can be equated with those others. Immensely useful though it is, the Museums Association is not in the same relationship to museum people as are the British Medical Association, the Law Society or the Royal Institute of British Architects to the professions over which they preside. All that can be said is that appropriate qualifications are required of a would-be entrant to any of the categories of post embraced by the profession, and that they are equivalent to the qualifications for comparable posts in other professions.

IX *Museums and the Universities*

THERE HAVE always been close relations between museums and the universities; but in fact those relations are as much in need of examination as those between museums and the rest of the community.

Sciences such as biology and anthropology have long regarded museum collections as essential sources of study material, and in addition most universities have built up collections of their own, many of which have developed into regular museums even in the sense of their being available to the general public. In the past such museums have tended to be little more than store-houses, and, even where there is public admission, curators—who are often members of the university staff—did not give a great deal of thought to presentation until comparatively recent times. The United States have been well to the forefront in new thinking about museums, yet there, too, there were university museums which made little concession to such thinking, places such as the Peabody Museum of Anthropology at Harvard where serried lines of flints or whatever it might be seemed to belong to a past age. One may accept the argument that a university museum is basically a library of teaching material and that curating this material is all that matters; but it is being recognized that this is a negative attitude, and that the museum can take a much more active part in the teaching system. One might instance the new Zoological Museum of Copenhagen University. This is an establishment with quite positive ideas about its role, where the needs of students are catered for at every level, with careful planning of working conditions, as in a modern library, and a lay-out bringing the student into close contact with high-level research. There is space available for public exhibitions, but this is secondary to the main purpose of the museum and separate from it.

What I am mainly concerned with here is the service which

public museums can perform for the universities, rather than the reverse, as university museums are primarily adjuncts of the teaching departments with which they are connected; but university museums do have a certain obligation to the community in general, especially since the universities became increasingly dependent upon public funds. This is perhaps specially true where art museums are concerned. Great works of art are part of the common heritage, and where they belong to what is virtually a public institution they should be available to those who wish to enjoy them. This has long been recognized by the universities. Museums such as the Ashmolean at Oxford and the Fitzwilliam at Cambridge are more or less public museums, and on the whole their methods of presentation recognize this, here and there with a bonus such as the special privilege of being able to tread on rare rugs which would not be normal in a typical public museum. Equally 'public', if at first sight they seem to be rather more part of the university precinct, are places like the Hunterian at Glasgow and the Gulbenkian Museum of Oriental Art at Durham. In the United States, where the universities have spent big sums of money on collecting expeditions, the public's familiarity with other cultures would be much poorer without, for example, the great South American collections of Philadelphia University or the Chinese collections of the Fogg at Harvard.

But only a few university collections are comparable with those of the larger public museums, and universities naturally make considerable use of those museums. There is continual intercourse of many sorts. Specimens, sometimes even entire sub-collections are lent to university specialists for long periods of time: an arrangement which is of mutual benefit, since the more a collection is worked upon the more valuable it becomes. However, there is room for more systematic use of those collections. Partly this may be the fault of the universities; but in the older museums reserve collections even now are sometimes difficult to refer to, because of out-of-date methods of storage which can make a search for the right specimen and cross-references to comparable specimens laborious to carry out. Modernization of methods has of course been going on for long enough and the best systems are familiar to museum staffs, but the transfer of collections to new-type accommodation is a lengthy and costly process which only institutions with considerable resources behind them can contemplate. Nor is it always easy to convince finance committees and similar controlling bodies of the importance of such expensive undertakings. What may be obvious to the trustee type of supervisor may not be equally obvious to a town councillor looking for tangible, value-for-money results. Storage and backroom activities, however impressive on paper, for the layman in such matters have not quite the appeal of spectacular displays in the public galleries or of schemes involving large numbers of school children. For all I have said against regarding museums as collections, it cannot be overstressed that the material in the collections is immensely valuable, yet such value is measurable only in terms of the knowledge which may be derived from them, and this is directly related to their availability.

What has been said in the last paragraph applies in the main to scientific collections. The use made by universities of reserve collections in the art museums is plainly widespread in a centre such as London, and it is growing. Here I think availability is less of a problem. In the art galleries, reserve paintings for the most part are easily accessible. As for the other art museums, new display methods for the primary halls and galleries are generally supported by secondary or study collections in which subjects are classified by materials and arranged chronologically under conditions which simplify use by students. Good use is made of such study collections. This applies not only to the universities but to the art colleges. It is my impression, however, that students from the art colleges could benefit a great deal more than they do from the museums, which they seem for the most part to regard as sources of subject matter rather than as introductions to other cultures, and it would add much to their development as practising artists if they were led to study the significance of what they are looking at. The problems of discipline in so many art colleges, and indeed the gulf in sympathy between the products of those colleges and the community at large, stems from the doctrine of art for art's sake, which no one who has made a study in any depth of the art of the past could accept. One meets so often students who, happily enough, are excited by the discovery of some unfamiliar piece of work, perhaps Indian or African or South American, but whose excitement is a purely visual titillation or is derived from a train of thought not justified by the conditions which produced the work they are looking at. Beauty is so much more than skin deep. A great deal of nonsense perpetrated today in the name of 'abstract' art would have been avoided if students had been disciplined by being required to understand the significance of the many manifestations of the abstract in the arts of ancient and of primitive peoples.

All I am asking is that study collections in the art museums should be taken as seriously as study collections in the scientific museums. Naturally they are so taken by students reading for an academic degree in the arts, but that is another matter. Where universities might perhaps give more thought to the art museums is in connection with courses such as history and geography and those involving the study of foreign cultures. So often there is insight to be gained about a period remote in time through examination of a few paintings or carvings or *objets d'art* which cannot come from the perusal of documents or the reading of books. The reign of Charlemagne may be a dark age indeed to some academic eyes, but emerges as something very different after an hour or two in the Cathedral Treasury at Aachen. Some peoples—the Celts, for example, or the Scyths— can scarcely be approached at all except through their art. For certain university courses the museum may be as important as the library.

Those universities which have courses in art history do of course make widespread use of the public institutions; but it may be asked whether they do not perhaps send their students to museums and galleries with objectives too limited by the scope of the curriculum and of the recommended reading when their eyes should be wide open to the full riches available. I am not blaming university teachers for this so much as those pressures which make a truly liberal education secondary to the passing of examinations. My comment stems from experience of candidates interviewed for posts in museums, honours graduates for most of whom art seems to mean painting and sculpture. Those young people have clearly made many visits to art galleries for every visit to a museum of decorative or applied art. The unfortunate division between the so-called 'fine arts' and the rest is something which the museums themselves will have to deal with, but meanwhile it is a question of proper direction of students. Things have improved considerably in recent years, partly perhaps because of the extraordinary increase of public interest in antiques and

87

antiquities; but the imbalance is still apparent, and with a strong bias towards the European field anyway. The result is that the small annual number of graduates who are our potential art historians and critics tend to be blinkered against experiences with which they should be familiar—and mention of critics reminds me that prominent newspaper art critics attending the Edinburgh International Festival have told me that they fight shy of even the most important exhibitions in spheres such as Byzantine art or Celtic art because they are not familiar with the background and feel they are not competent to make assessments. The great masters of European painting and sculpture were, after all, thrown up by epochs seething with talent in many arts and with craft skills which are nearly unimaginable in a machine-dominated age. Our young graduates are well aware of this. But their familiarity with actual examples of painting is seldom matched by a comparable familiarity with the wood-carvings, the goldsmiths' work, the glass and ceramics, the masterpieces of weaving—things which often enough are reflected in the paintings themselves. As for the world of oriental art, in many respects so much more sophisticated than our own, it is a closed book to most of them. Some could not hazard a reasonable guess as to whether a Han bronze or a Ming jar was the older. Such narrow learning would not, I think, be acceptable in a history or a classics graduate. In the United States matters are perhaps rather better. If so, I suspect some at least of the credit can go to the museums, which are not only rich in oriental art but often lay emphasis upon it, and not infrequently recruit Chinese, Japanese and Indian scholars to their staffs. This is no more than an indication of how museums may exert a liberal influence on the scope of the university education.

Fuller use of museums as indicated poses the question of teaching responsibilities on the side of the museums. Improved availability of the collections is not the whole answer. Interpretation cannot be left entirely to university staff. Quite frequently the authority in some branch of study will be a senior member of the museum staff, and although he may not be called upon to lecture or demonstrate regularly, it is right that he should be available to students just as their professors, lecturers and tutors are. This will have to be kept in mind when new museum office and laboratory blocks are designed: availability of staff is as

important as availability of the collections. This may scarcely
seem to be worth mentioning, but in the old-fashioned museum
it has sometimes been difficult for the most determined visitor
to make contact with the keeper or assistant-keeper he wanted to
meet; he would find himself conducted through a labyrinth of
passages with doors unlocked and locked again behind him as if
he were visiting a convict in a top-security prison. The diffident
student interprets such inaccessibility as something more than
physical. In an institution like the Copenhagen museum referred
to, the scientists are placed in logical proximity to their collections
and there are study-rooms where supervision can be conducted
with minimal difficulty. Such a lay-out facilitates too the takeover of certain teaching duties by museum staff, at least for small
groups of students such as those engaged on post-graduate studies.
In this last connection, it would seem quite reasonable to suggest
that responsibility for Ph.D. students in appropriate cases should
be handed over to museum staff. Here again one tends to think
in terms of the scientific disciplines, zoology, for example, or
palaeontology. Yet there is an equally good case for advanced
studies in art subjects on occasion becoming the responsibility
of authorities in museums who even now may become involved
as outside examiners or in some consultative capacity.

Such an area of academic work as taxonomy—the classification
of material, particularly natural history material—in the main
has become a museum responsibility, as conservation of material
has been for long enough. Time was when eminent scientists, in
universities and elsewhere, were content to collect and describe
in the tradition of Linnaeus, and a man could usefully spend his
life with net and notebook pushing back the frontiers of knowledge. Most of this type material found its way into museums. Not
a few scientists in museums today are willing that universities
should leave this sort of work to them, enabling the universities
to be that much more free for pure research. At first sight this
may seem a fair division of labour, but I think it is a situation
which museums should be cautious about accepting in their
plans for future development. Indeed, one might cast doubts on
whether there is much of a future in it for them at all. Certainly
they must be assiduous in curating their collections; but Coleman
quoting Alexander G. Ruthven on university museums, long ago
uttered a warning about museums 'overdoing' taxonomy. 'It is a

curiosity of systematic zoology to-day', Ruthven writes, 'that not a few systematists seem to regard papers announcing changes in names as contributions to science.' And he goes on: 'Nothing can be more sad than the spectacle of a trained zoologist allowing the search for prior names to absorb a considerable amount of his time.'

That museums should be content with this kind of custodian-ship of their collections is as stultifying as their remaining content with the old-fashioned idea of a public gallery or with the case-by-case inventory type of publication. To accept such a role as a main function would certainly insure an academic staff of third-rate capacity. The main issues in scholarship in museums are much the same as those in universities, with certain differences of emphases. One cannot help wondering whether directors and senior keepers in our great museums are vigilant enough in their scrutiny of the work of their staffs to guard against too much time spent on the accumulation of minor information leading nowhere in particular; but then one may wonder also if the heads of departments in some of our universities are any more vigilant! Research of the right sort is an inspiration in any institution concerned with advanced education. If museums are to play their part in such advanced education they must constantly review with critical eyes the quality of the work going on in their 'backrooms' and make sure that, ultimately at least, it will have its contribution to make to the main stream of progress in the world outside.

An obvious subject for consideration is the Open University. One may have one's reservations about the necessity for such a venture. For myself, I am opposed to the proliferation of universities today on the ground that the province of higher education has been debased by a materialistic outlook which sees the university merely as a vocational training college. The Open University, however, may be something else. It is aimed not at the products of the schools, themselves expanded by the raising of the leaving age, but at a previous generation, at those who feel they have been deprived of further education for one reason or another, even at those who in later life feel a need for 're-education'.

This ambitious project must necessarily have a very long experimental stage. If money is available, it is relatively easy to plan and set up a complex of buildings round a campus and to recruit a body of professors and lecturers to devise and offer academic courses on well-established lines. It is a very different matter to offer similar courses to men and women living at home up and down the country, people who can have no sense of belonging to a corporate body with all the advantages of intercourse and advice and precedent inherent in such a body. This problem is being met by the provision of study centres where people can meet together, take part in discussions and develop a feeling of identity. These are being housed in existing educational institutions. There has been discussion about the inclusion of museums among such institutions.

I must confess to some astonishment that the use of museums for such centres was not put forward at a very early stage in discussions about the Open University project, because it seems to me that for certain branches of teaching no other institution is so manifestly right for the purpose. Surely if the Open University had any requirement that was more clamant than the need for a feeling of being corporate, it was the need for a place where students could actually see and have first-hand experience of the material things which were being talked about. For instance, technological advances and the need to understand what they were all about were, so I believe, one of the main factors which influenced the formation of the Open University. One of the principal channels of instruction is television and a great deal can be learned by this means; but instruction through one of the mass media alone can never compensate for lack of the conditions enjoyed by students at universities and technical colleges where all necessary equipment is provided. Yet it would not take a great sum of money in terms of University Grants Committee expenditure to provide the major museums of this country with facilities for instructing groups of students of the Open University in the practical application of principles, using their existing resources of technological and scientific material, and with the whole range of the museum's collections at hand to reinforce any special display set up in the instruction centre. What is true for the sciences and technology is equally true for the arts. Art history is one of the subjects offered by the Open University, and although here again a great deal can be done through television it would be absurd to compare the television image with the real thing, even if colour sets were available to students, which in most cases they would not be. A small selection of images on a television screen can provide only the most rudimentary instruction, and where sculpture and objects in the round are concerned it is essential sooner or later that opportunities to handle must supplement visual impressions.

Finally, I would say that a link between the Open University and museums would be an opportunity for education of a wide cross-section of the intelligent public in the right use of museums. It has always been a problem with museums that their undoubtedly huge public is something of an amorphous mass, drifting in and out, always difficult to keep in contact with, often indifferent to the significance of what they are looking at. The students of the Open University seem to be drawn from just that section of the public most eager to benefit from what the museums have to offer. They are neither the 'prepared students' of an ordinary university, nor are they what Coleman calls the 'everchanging representation of the unprepared' which is the museum's normal clientèle; and if by systematic instruction within the walls of the museum they can be made familiar with one or more of the disciplines covered by the museum, eventually they will have on the general museum-going public an influence of considerable importance. They might be expected to lead that public in attendances at special exhibitions or other enterprises, they might well form the core of lecture-attenders, they will probably head the demands for new publications. Museums are like so many other democratic institutions. Whether they can be made to work as they should is entirely dependent on popular education. The Open University would seem to be intended as the successor of the Workers' Educational Association and those other nineteenth-century organizations which aimed to close the gap between the masses and the privileged élite which once ruled in the name of the people. Just as those bodies popularized the use of public libraries, so the Open University could help to revolutionize the use of museums.

X *Museums and the Schools*

SINCE THE last war a great deal has been thought and written about the value of visual education, but relationships between museums and the schools have not really done as much as they might to implement this. Partly it may be due to the fact that museums and schools tend to be large, committed and in some degree conservative institutions. A revolutionary new relationship would be costly in money and effort, even if anyone could agree about what direction it should take. Therefore, although schools services in museums have in general over a span of thirty years been transformed quantitatively, and indeed also in the quality of the work done, we are still waiting for the real break-through which could make the store of knowledge locked in our museums readily available to young people in a big way.

About the beginning of our thirty-year period Herbert Read wrote profoundly and persuasively on the part which should be played by art in the education of the whole child (*Education Through Art*). He is mainly concerned with the practice of art, with the development of personality and the capacity to originate. What he and others wrote at this time has had its effect, and the age of laborious copying of objects in the art rooms of primary schools is long past. To some extent it has even had an effect upon what is done when classes visit museums. There is much more freedom for the individual child to follow up what interests him, certainly to select what he wants to draw or paint; but such visits still tend to be few in any one year for a child, and I suspect the value of them depends largely on the interest and understanding of the teachers involved. The impact of the museum on the mind of a child at primary stage should be profound. How profound can be seen by anyone observing a visit by handicapped children, especially blind children, for whom some museums provide special facilities, as all museums should be in a position to do. The understanding of the blind

D   93 child can be watched growing as he handles a small animal or a simple piece of machinery. Here is a child suddenly introduced to something which has been a mere name to him, and his excitement is only matched by his capacity to recognize the significance of what his touch tells him. A similar excitement, although unhappily not the same swift reaction, may be seen when spastic children are brought into contact with what the museum has to offer.

These responses are in marked contrast to those of too many normal schoolchildren in organized visits. In a sense the so-called normal child's perception has been blunted just because it has not been deprived, in our times perhaps blunted by over-indulgence, not only in the home but also in schools which are often equipped and financed on a scale unthinkable a couple of generations ago. Perhaps what the 'normal' child *is* deprived of is a sense of wonder. Its television screens ensure that nothing is unfamiliar to it, and familiarity without real knowledge breeds contempt. The contempt may in turn be one of the breeders of vandalism, and it is significant that vandalism by young people in museums has increased enormously since the war. Before the war it was rare. To my mind it is one of the most important tasks facing the museum educational service to foster in the normal child the same spirit of wonder and excitement which it is so pathetically easy to engender in the handicapped child, and if the modern environment is as hostile to this as I think it is, then museums must make a positive and forceful effort to help redress the balance.

I am concerned here only with the schools, but in passing it should be emphasized that—unless children have changed entirely since I was small—no organized school visit will ever stir the sense of the marvellous as leisure-time visits by the individual child will. For this reason I believe it is essential to keep a close watch on how regulations excluding children 'unaccompanied by an adult' are carried out by security staff. I am well aware of the many problems involved in this aspect of security, but I am also aware of the value of the hundreds of entrancing hours which I spent alone in museums and galleries as a child.

There is a much closer link between museums and primary schools than there is with secondary schools, and I will say something about this first. Here progress is, broadly, on two fronts. There is no doubt that the museum plays a more active part than it once did. In former times it did little more than open its doors to school parties, which had to make what they could, or what their teachers could, of the collections, whereas now the museum, where it can, tries to supply an educational service of its own. American museums have had fully organized education departments for a long time, for example at the Metropolitan in New York and the National Gallery in Washington, and in Britain the Glasgow Museum and Art Galleries have led in this field, although it should be noted that the remarkable little museum at Haslemere in Surrey was founded as an educational museum as early as 1895. Travelling exhibitions such as those organized by the Science Museum and the National Museum of Wales are welcomed by schools, and possession of an education department or at least of full-time educational staff is now common in this country.

The other area which has seen a marked advance is that of child participation, as against ordinary instruction. Ever since museums began to instal working models operated by the visitor by means of press-buttons, the fascination of these for children has been shown. This is the next best thing to handling, and even that is sometimes possible. Far too much of our education has been and still is on an intellectual level. Sensory communication is far more effective for certain aspects of basic learning, and although visually exhibits in glass cases are an advance on books and blackboards, an element of unreality remains. The importance of manual experience is seen in the child's instinct to grasp at everything it sees. Handling plainly is not possible with most of the things we see in museum cases, but often there is much secondary material which might be handled under supervision. The Geffrye Museum, which has done so much to pioneer work with children, enables them even to wear some of the period costumes. Another form of participation now common is the drawing or painting class, with or without free choice of subject. One thinks of this as an art class, but primarily it is a function of visual education, for the child is drawn closer to the subject by his own efforts. There is also increased use of what might now be called 'feed-back', in the shape of checks and questionnaires. Something of the sort is necessary to ensure that the right information is getting across. But at the same time, it is important that the child should not lose the feeling that the museum is a place where his mind can adventure in new fields, and questionnaires should be framed to encourage him to express freely his own reactions. This is particularly true in the case of art museums.

Extra-mural museum activities are an important part of all this. They can help to offset in the earliest years that misconception of the museum as a building rather than a centre of activity, something which I have criticized in another chapter. Especially I have in mind expeditions. These have been organized for a long time by many museums on both sides of the Atlantic, usually as a week-end or holiday activity voluntarily attended, but they might usefully be incorporated under the general head of school visits. Perhaps the commonest purpose of such expeditions has been nature-study, with visits to archaeological or historic sites now also coming into the picture. Right thinking about the arts demands that young people be shown that those also do not belong only within the four walls of a gallery. The impression that art is some kind of exclusive cult only to be enjoyed by initiates must be killed early, before instinctive pleasure in it is dulled, and museums could do much to show it is an essential element in human effort in humble callings as well as the studios of great masters and to direct attention to the amenities of the ordinary scene. It is important too that children should early get the 'feel' of the pure joy of making things, once part of the inheritance of the craftsman everywhere and tragically now so rarely experienced. They could be helped by visits to workshops and studios. A child who has seen glass blown or a silver bowl raised or a pot turned on a wheel or a pattern emerging from the play of shuttles on a loom has a new interest in the end-products of all those processes or of related crafts, and is some way along the road towards understanding techniques which made possible the masterpieces in the galleries. More important, such a child has had implanted in him some notion of the idea of quality which, like the inculcation of moral judgement, is a necessary part of the fitting of a young man or woman to play a responsible rôle in society.

But the most formidable part of the problem of how to draw schools and museums closer is to discover how museums can help in secondary education. It is doubtful if any serious progress has been made in studies to this end either in this country or in any in the Western world, including America, in the last decade or two, although the report of a working party set up by the Trustees of the British Museum recommended that there should be concentration on 'the needs of senior pupils in secondary schools and on higher education in all its forms'. In a society where paper qualifications seem to count for more and more the examination system for school-leavers is increasingly demanding; and although it must be agreed that teaching methods for senior pupils, especially on the science side, are far more efficient than they once were, curricula become tighter. I think that so far as intellectually bright pupils are concerned results are remarkable. However, those belong to an élite. I very much doubt if the ordinary pupil of the secondary school, splendidly equipped for teaching though it may be, is better educated than his father was. He seems to be less contented, more liable to become a social problem, and this tendency must increase after the raising of the school-leaving age. The Devil is on the look-out for idle brains even more than for idle hands. The problem of 'submerged' secondary pupils obviously is one which will have to be tackled in a big way by the schools themselves, and the threat of child trade-unionism and 'pupil-power' is going to increase in parallel to troubles stemming from lack of work-satisfaction in industry and the wider world. Most discontent of this kind stems from frustrated creativity, from lack of involvement with work which is in itself rewarding. This I believe to be one of the great challenges to modern society, and it is one which most of our leaders prefer to ignore or to hide behind reassurances about higher living standards. In face of such a challenge it almost seems like bathos to revert to museums; but if one confines the challenge to the non-academic stream of young people in the schools, museums can perhaps do a considerable amount to help meet it. I recall some years ago addressing a youth club in a fairly tough new housing estate on the subject of museums. Far from being the ordeal I anticipated, the occasion provided one of the most receptive audiences I have ever had the privilege of speaking to. Unlike a middle-aged audience, those youths and girls needed no conversion to the idea that collecting and sorting out and re-habilitating relics of past ages was an interesting thing to do and

97

several of them at the end wanted to know how they could get out of their present employment and into a museum. To those young people conditioned to conveyor-belts and office filing-systems, artifacts from ancient Egypt or Red Indian territory or the Industrial Revolution held a strong appeal.

It is unnecessary to emphasize the practical difficulties of any attempt to bring together pupils and museums on such a scale as to make the experiment worth while. Not least is the recruitment of the right men and women on the museum side. It is not a matter of transferring teachers to the museum service. If they are to stir the interest of pupils who are there for the negative reason that they are not academically inclined, they have to be natural interpreters—people so committed to and excited by their subject that their enthusiasm is catching. The aim is to put flesh on the bones of history, physics, anthropology, biology and other disciplines, to give such studies purpose for pupils who feel they are mere obstacles to their freedom to seek jobs and earn a living.

The part which museums could play in preparing pupils for the higher examinations should not need to be stressed, but in fact it has scarcely been considered seriously, and is not mentioned except as a passing reference to access to reserve collections among suggestions for the future in the report, *Museums in Education* (1971). When one considers how much progress there has been in developing the modern museum, it is astonishing that the link with the schools is confined almost entirely to the elementary and junior secondary level. I have discussed this with directors of education and have had meetings with groups of senior and specialist teachers, and there has always been agreement that museums have much to offer to secondary pupils. The stumbling-block has been the logistics of the problem. Curricula are tight. Transport of pupils to museums could be time-consuming. But perhaps the biggest difficulty is that the museums must provide specialist teaching staff to demonstrate and interpret the material and to co-ordinate with the schools, and times have not been propitious for staff increases on the necessary scale.

Initially one is always asked: what has the museum to offer the pupil? The most evident possibilities lie in such fields as physics and biology. Schools now carry the study of science subjects considerably further than they did in my young days. Their teaching requirements therefore are more complex. Elaborate apparatus beyond the means of most individual schools might be assembled in suites of study-rooms in museums, in some cases even in the public galleries, and remain permanently in being to be demonstrated to visiting schools by specialist staff. Some believe that because this is not in line with the museum's traditional functions it would be better located in centres under the control of the education authority; but in fact some museums—museums of technology and science—are building displays of this kind all the time, as indeed they must do if they are to interpret what is happening today as well as what happened yesterday. The larger scientific museums in Europe and America mount elaborate displays, often very sophisticated, and they possess incomparable 'know-how' to enable them to develop such displays. Lesser museums naturally are some way behind; but often this is only relative and because funds are not available, and they too sometimes have the basic knowledge which they could expand upon rapidly, given staff and money. In the field of biology the position is the same. The old attitude which rested content with corridors of stuffed animals and birds is a thing of the past, and in many major institutions collections are being re-deployed to illustrate problems of ecology, environment, conservation. Here again, to bend the effort to meet the needs of senior school pupils would mean additional resources. I think that if the need were for more laboratory facilities in the schools themselves it would be accepted in principle, even if the money were not immediately available.

What museums might do for the secondary pupil in arts subjects may not be so obvious, yet in my meetings with the specialist teachers I was impressed with the number who saw opportunities in precisely those subjects. The teaching of history and geography has no doubt changed as much as the teaching of science. For one thing, those subjects are no longer linked to the imperial tradition, which undoubtedly coloured the teaching of them even after the 1914–18 war. Clive's victories now are less important than the ethnology and economics of the sub-continent, and some museums are as well-equipped to demonstrate those as they are to demonstrate the application of atomic energy. For nearly a century storage space has been loaded with

99

the loot of colonial campaigns from Ashanti to New Zealand, and with the harvests of missionary zeal. Some might even see it as a matter of conscience to use these things as teaching material to enlighten new generations about the basic problems and cultures and aspirations of peoples who are again confronting us in a shrinking world. And the material also could be used to teach Asian and West Indian children about their own cultures, and so to promote interracial understanding.

Then as to the visual arts: their significance is at last beginning to be recognized, and art teaching is no longer mere instruction in how to draw an apple or paint a vase of flowers. Art history and aesthetics are now available subjects, and they cannot be taught without constant recourse to original works of art. What I would press for here again, not for the only time in this book, is that art studies should not be confined to the fine arts. It is especially important to see the arts as a whole in school, when attitudes are still in process of formation. Also I believe the approach to art is much more natural for young people if made through the avenues of craft-skills which are, after all, the basis of all art. And it is not merely at the elementary stage that pupils respond more readily to principles inherent in functional objects than when they are confronted with a daunting major work. Such an apparently abstract notion as empathy is in no way mysterious to a boy or girl with a Venetian wine-glass or a Cominazzo pistol in front of them, better still in their grasp. Another limitation which should be disposed of, especially for those reading for advanced level examinations, is the confining of art teaching to the European field. Our great collections of the decorative arts of the East in particular would open up a new dimension for the young student, but here the museum's own specialist staff would certainly have to assist.

In a paper read to a conference in Russia in 1968, Mrs B. James describes the importance of 'experience' in education. She was referring to the sort of encounter which opens the eyes of an individual to beauty or some other quality, and which results in 'personal involvement and commitment'. It is what in religion would be called a revelation. The experience which concerns her relates to excellence, and where better to look for it, she asks, than in our treasure-houses, the museums? It happens involuntarily to certain children, usually perhaps the more sensitive and gifted ones, in their private wanderings around galleries and museums. It could happen much more often, to more ordinarily-endowed children; but Mrs James wisely pointed out it does not just happen, but needs the skill of a teacher and much time, support and encouragement, and she goes on to underline the importance of care in planning, delicacy of touch, and a personal welcome. As far as schoolchildren are concerned, to anyone trying to cope with the crowded curricula of today this may sound like an impossible ideal, but it is an ideal which both schools and museums should be vigilant in keeping before them. The introduction of a child to a museum can be critical. It demands very special qualities in museum staff, among them deep sensibility. Duncan F. Cameron, in a paper on 'Museums in the Contemporary World', refers to the child's search for its own identity in collecting things about him, and to the reality of the small world so created which a grown-up often so unthinkingly destroys by tidying it up. The museum can offer such a world. It must always be something other than a schoolroom. From the first it must be an experience, the start of numberless avenues of exploration leading out of sight over the horizon.

XI *The Present Dichotomy*

CURRENT THINKING about museums has produced in some minds a rather uncomfortable dilemma. The horns of this dilemma are, on the one hand, conservation and research, and on the other education, and to quite a number of people they appear to be divergent. Those who see the two functions of museums like this ponder the need to split them into two types of institution, or wonder whether one function should be transferred to another sort of institution.

This is not a matter for mere idle speculation. It is an everyday, practical problem. Most directors of large museums know the difficulties it gives rise to in staffing, for example. Senior staff are tending to split into two streams. In the days when staffs were relatively small there was no great difficulty, because those attracted to museum work tended to be of a certain type of man or woman, a type interested mainly in collecting, who might or might not have had university education but enjoyed amassing knowledge and often also enjoyed passing it on, after a fashion, by laying out and labelling the collections in the public galleries. In those days a director might have to accept that A was keen on field work, B was a bit of a recluse who rarely emerged from his study, C spent his time writing books or papers on the material in his charge and D was actually enthusiastic about arranging displays for the public. All categories except B had their uses, and B one simply had to put up with. The best curator, of course, was a combination of A, C and D. In the museums, it was a time of splendid amateurism, although great names emerged from this rather unprofessional set-up.

I have a deep respect for the amateur, and I am sure we are going to regret his passing, in every realm including sport. Many of our great museums had their characters moulded by those dedicated enthusiasts whose rewards were certainly not to be measured in terms of material gain. Some—one thinks of retired clergymen devoting themselves to, say, this or that genus of Lepidoptera—were not even on the pay-roll at all and made no name for themselves except perhaps the single entry '*var. purpureus* (Smith)' in an obscure check-list. But all those strangely-assorted people were held together by the very eccentricity of their calling and no one felt constrained to divide them into sheep and goats or to assess their varying degrees of usefulness. Such haphazard recruitment is a thing of the past. Museums, like other professions, are becoming compartmentalized, and the compartments group themselves in two broad clusters, those concerned with the collections and research, and those concerned with the public galleries and everything that comes under the head of education. Inevitably there is competition: for money, for territory, for new staff. Not a few of the academic staff in some museums would welcome the setting up of research institutions independent of the museums.

Is such a split a practical possibility? Expense apart, there is no particular reason why reserve and study collections should not be removed from the larger museums and re-housed with the required laboratories and workrooms under separate roofs. They would go into buildings of functional design, planned for efficient running, by contrast with the present accommodation for research work which too often is still relegated to cellars and attics and antiquated annexes inadequately adapted. Not only would collections be more readily available for specialist students, but conservation also would be simpler than it is in old buildings with rambling halls and galleries where air-conditioning, for instance, is extremely costly or even impossible to introduce. Alternatively, the material for public display could undergo the re-housing. It could be given the advantage of presentation under ideal conditions, with no need to try to insert streamlined modern cases and carefully controlled lighting into Victorian gothic or neo-classical interiors, and with lecture-theatres, classrooms and all the other adjuncts of educational programmes appropriately positioned. Indeed it is likely neither side would wish to be left in possession of the original building! The big dispute, of course, would be over the collections themselves. There would be strong objection to the abstraction of much of the finest material from the immediate control of research staff, and yet in the case of art museums at least it could not be avoided. And there would be good reason for the objection on several grounds, especially if academic staff had ceased to have control of conditions under which the material would be displayed. Yet the right to interfere would complicate the problem of splitting the functions of museum and research establishment. The educational staff of the museum would be frustrated by removal of all but limited groups of objects from easy access. And there are many other complications. Therefore, while a physical division of the institutions may seem relatively simple, it is doubtful if the advantages would offset the disadvantages.

If I devote more space to the case for the *status quo* it is because there is no doubt in my mind that it is right to retain it, but also because the retention of what may seem to be rather unwieldly institutions needs justification.

An objection to division which at first sight looks merely sentimental is loss of identity. The British Museum would not be the same place if the bulk of the collections were transferred to somewhere in the suburbs and a research institute set up there. Indeed the proposal to remove the Library and Reading Room to another site where they would become a National Library independent of the Museum roused a massive protest. The reason for the protest in the main, of course, was not sentiment, but the threat to a circumstance which is unique: the integration of one of the world's greatest libraries with one of its greatest collections of archaeology and art. It is easy to argue that such close integration is unnecessary. The equivalent libraries in Wales, Scotland and Ireland are not bound up with national museums, nor have the Bibliothéque Nationale and the Library of Congress any such associations. But the British Museum, like many another long-established place of learning, is more than bricks and mortar, and I believe that one should look very long before drastically interfering with any such institution. The application of cold reason to the planning of human affairs has resulted in enough disastrous errors to suggest that we rarely know all the factors involved when we begin to calculate. The factor of identity, a strange mixture of traditions and customs and even prejudices, can be as subtly important in a museum as in a university.

Greater efficiency and better conditions for research if functions were split have been mentioned, but I am not altogether convinced that the quality of research would improve. Even under present arrangements it is all too easy for research staff to enter into a kind of cloistered scholasticism, study for the sake of study. It is never easy to co-ordinate and direct research, and if the only goal is the 'improvement' of large collections of material by classification and cross-referencing and adding innumerable small pieces of information, often in the pious hope that someone some day will find it useful, there is a danger that a high proportion of staff engaged in this work will end up by wasting their own time and the public's money. It takes a strong-minded man to steer a reasonably straight course under such circumstances. Not that the fact that he has certain public duties, and may even be sought out for consultation by an importunate member of the public, will save a man under the present system from becoming an ostrich; but at least he does keep rubbing shoulders with colleagues with widely-varying views about their responsibilities, and this must have its effect. He is part of an institution with recognized aims, aims of which his superiors at least are conscious, and he is open to frequent cross-examination, however casual, about the end-purpose of what he is doing. To learn more and more about less and less until one knows everything about nothing of importance is more easily achieved in certain museum fields than it could be in, say, the research department of a great medical establishment or the pharmaceutical industry, but even the museum backroom boy is subject to constant reminders of his employers' obligations to the community.

Conversely, divorce between research and educational functions of the museums could be fully as harmful in its effect on the public galleries and all instructional work. A museum, as I have stressed earlier, is so much more than a shop-window display. The display staff who are now increasing so fast in numbers and importance, even more the longer existing specialist craftsmen such as taxidermists, engineers and restorers, are the first to know the difference between working for a commercial interest whose only purpose is to boost sales—some display staff are recruited from industry—and working for an institution with academic standards to which they also must conform. It is the difference between ephemeral and lasting satisfaction in one's work. Not many jobs offer this sort of satisfaction today. Not that the standards required by a purely educational museum would be lower than those set by museum authorities, but in any museum which prides itself on its academic excellence new displays on the galleries come under constant criticism from academic staff sensitive to misinterpretation of their subjects. In fact, in course of time display and other specialist staff are in some degree influenced by what in current jargon might be called the 'think-tank' working on the collections from which they draw their material, and this pressure upon them renders them more critical of their own work and eventually vastly increases their standard of performance. This also applies of course to guide-lecturers and all staff employed to interpret collections to the public or to schools. If at any time they can refer back to authoritative opinion they will be more effective than if their authorities were comparative strangers to them; and if their utterances on the galleries or in the lecture-hall can be overheard by such authorities or reported to them they will be less liable to make unconsidered assertions on controversial points.

The twin functions of our greater museums as at present constituted seem, therefore, to be an essential element in the effectiveness and authority of the work of the museums as a whole.

How best to harness the two functions together is a problem which varies from museum to museum. Some directors probably do not recognize there is a problem at all or may even not need to recognize it, others would give it very high priority. That it is of high priority I have no doubt myself. There is plenty of sound philosophy in the museum profession, but politics, finance and other things act as a drag on its becoming effective, and any major doubt as to what museums are all about plays into the hands of those who would like to give them very low priority indeed. The demands of both museum functions have grown greater with the increased sophistication of research methods and educational requirements, and it is essential to iron out conflict of interest where it occurs.

I suspect this chapter sounds a little unreal to the layman in such matters, and it might be useful at this point to move from the general to the particular and to break down the problem and how it may be tackled in a specific case. I have already (in Chapter IV, 'The Museum is not a Building') referred to a project for a hall of biology in my former museum. It is a good example of the smooth working of the research and visual education functions of the museum in a combined operation. Basically, the theme was the nature of life itself. I pick on this project primarily because research in this field is not so slow-moving as in some others and because significant discoveries are relatively frequent, so that the danger of 'freezing' a display too soon, of committing the museum to a series of assertions some of which might be negated by a new discovery, is quite a possibility. There could be a similar situation with a 'permanent' display of space exploration. Obviously the museum has to commit itself at some point or the hall would never be completed; but the more open the line of communication between senior research staff in touch with progress on the one hand and, on the other, the technical and display staff responsible for the gallery itself, the more valid will be the final result. This is especially important when, as in the case in point, the display staff were co-operating with a team of display specialists in London, 400 miles away. There is an element of exaggeration in that what I have said, in so far as it is unlikely that so revolutionary a discovery would be made as to demand the wholesale scrapping of plans; but it is no exaggeration to say the academic staff would not have been satisfied with the result if they had been unable to influence it right up to the final stage. Moreover, such an exercise has a reassuring and stimulating effect which makes it easier to turn to other projects.

Coleman recognized the essential unity of the two functions when he wrote that 'museums are likely to be as deep or as shallow in their teaching as they are strong or weak in research.' Writing four years later his fellow-countryman A. E. Parr said: 'Original research is . . . both the inspiration and the measuring-rod of higher education.' Those are arguments against the division of academic staff into strictly-defined research and teaching departments, however well integrated these might be. In our national scientific museums there is a practice of grading staff in a way which must, I feel, emphasize the research function at the expense of the teaching one, for to classify a man or a woman as a scientific officer or a principal scientific officer must tend to weaken his identification with the museum service since it aligns him with his similarly-graded colleagues outside. I will not expand on this because I have no close experience of how it works out in practice, and I *do* know from experience that there are many scientific officers who are dedicated museum men; yet with such a title on your door is there not a temptation to close it against the pressures of lay events in the outside world? There is a good deal in a name. In my view, the older titles of keeper and assistant-keeper usual in art and other museums are more appropriate to the nature of the work, and if anyone is in doubt of their academic dignity let him remember the long list of distinguished authorities who have held posts with those gradings, many of them men and women whose reputation in the research field is matched by their brilliance as teachers—teachers, of course, in the widest sense. The dual-capacity museum man must not go. However much the need for staff rationalization, we must not make it more difficult for teaching staff to follow up lines of research which interest them or for the backroom men to develop abilities which they may have for teaching. In some museum circles this may seem like a prescription for chaos. But old-fashioned though it appears, I believe a measure of this flexibility is important if museums are to retain their special character.

Coleman almost dismisses the art museums of his country *qua* research institutions. Things are very different in the United States today. In the past thirty years or so the rich American collections have drawn to them from abroad some of the world's most distinguished art historians, men like W. G. Constable and Ananda Coomaraswamy, and they have bred many native historians of like distinction. In the United Kingdom there is a longer tradition, and I should be inclined to cite our larger art museums as examples of how easily research and education may be co-ordinated under one roof. In the arts as in other disciplines there are moles among post-graduate students, men and women whose preoccupation with minutiae blinds them to the vision and wider appeal of the artist who interests them; but by its very nature art stirs responses in its students which compel them to try to persuade others to see what they see and feel what they feel. Such people are natural museum material. The scientific disciplines are so much more objective. It is possible for a student of, say, the Coleoptera or Diptera legitimately to spend years at his microscope with one or two drawers of specimens beside him. Indeed I recall a friend who asserted he was going off for a sabbatical year to Berkeley taking his study-material with him in a pillbox in his waistcoat pocket! The end-result of this year-long concentration may well have been conclusions about the *anopheles* mosquito of vital importance to the checking of malaria, but it could hardly be a milestone on the road to better museums.

The nature of research in most art fields is such that it promotes contact with a wide variety of people and demands some knowledge of the world, even if it is mainly the art world. The most junior of assistant-keepers or curators in an art museum explores not merely the resources of his own collections but the attics and strong-rooms of remote country houses and dealers' back-premises, has to learn how to compete for prizes in the auction-rooms, and will often spend his vacations following trails into foreign cities and villages. Not only is he acquiring scholarship: he is also probably acquiring a certain *savoir faire* and becoming more articulate. The result of his researches may be anything from a modest addition to the collections to a major international exhibition. In short, his learning cannot but enhance the teaching capability of his museum in some degree. In such a museum a real dichotomy of function is nearly unthinkable. It should be no different in other sorts of museum. The material of a geological museum embraces the whole of the world we live in, of a natural history museum all living things in that world, of a technological museum all the tools of man and all he has created with them. Learning about these things and teaching about them is at least as much a follow-through process as learning about and teaching about the arts.

XII *Who Should Run Our Museums?*

ALREADY IT has been suggested (in Chapter IV, 'The Museum is not a Building') that a museum may in itself be a work of art, as well as a repository of art. One thinks of such places as Louisiana—the little gallery of modern painting in a garden at Humlebæk in Denmark—or of Colonial Williamsburg in Virginia; but creative artistry can and should even enter into modification of the older and less adaptable foundations if they are to elicit a good response from the community. The direction of museums, therefore, and especially the directorship, calls for additional qualities quite other than administrative. Somewhere at the top there has to be an urge to create. It has to be an urge so dominant that it will have the strength to demolish the sort of opposition which comes, not from reasoned criticism, but from the niggling conservatism and lack of vision which for so long too often have been obstacles to progress in museums.

This must sound like a rather extreme view. Clearly it cannot seriously be suggested that a top man should be able to impose his ideas on a public institution without there being some reasonable safeguards. Ultimate responsibility must lodge in a governing body of some kind. A museum or gallery is, after all, like a bank, the possessor of great wealth, whether it comes from public or private sources, and is maintained and developed with public or private money. As a bank has its board of directors formed of men of experience and weight who must be persuaded to concur before any major proposal can go forward, so a museum needs a board both knowledgeable and responsible to keep an eye on the use made of its treasures, whether artistic or scientific, and its funds. In this country there is a wide range of such boards or governing bodies. Some of the national museums are administered directly by Government departments, others through trustees. Municipal museums are of course the responsibility of local authorities. Universities control their own museums. Some smaller museums are under private bodies. On the continent the situation is roughly similar, but with differences of emphasis: for example in France the Louvre watches over the whole country through a director of museums located there, in Germany there is a strong municipal and regional organization in the Stadtmuseum and the Landesmuseum. In the United States, the great city museums tend to outrival the national museums, which are confined to Washington, and much more direct responsibility lies with private bodies, either through supporting membership or through benevolent individuals, as at Colonial Williamsburg or Winterthur.

Such variety among governing bodies makes for variety of outlook in the museums. It is to be hoped that uniformity will never descend upon them, that there will never be a rigid centralized control, either direct or fiscal. It is hard enough to live down the old museum image; we do not want to be faced with a recognizable museum pattern wherever there is a museum, large or small.

What concerns us here is how the governing bodies function, and whether they need to be modified in any way to ensure not only greater efficiency in the museum service but a readier response to the advances in museology which have been taking place over the past few decades. It would be intolerable if industrial boards of management closed their ears and eyes to relevant technological progress, and sooner or later shareholders would demand resignations if they grew aware of such indifference to their interests; but for the most part the 'shareholders' of our museums are the ratepayers and taxpayers, who are not particularly watchful of their interests and certainly unaware of what they can do about it if those interests are not being served.

First, it should be said the standard of service of the various types of governing body on the whole have improved out of all recognition. I have never worked in a local authority museum, but I have frequently heard those of my colleagues who have complaining that their committees—a 'Parks and Galleries Committee', even a 'Parks, Galleries and Cemeteries Committee'—have opposed some modest piece of expenditure on a painting or sculpture which the members could not comprehend. Nor is philistinism in local authority committees the only manifestation of the kind. Knowledgeable and scholarly boards of trustees too can have their prejudices, as when rigid classical tradition prompted them to oppose spending money on acquisitions other than Greek or Roman antiquities. Not that such conservatism is wholly reprehensible. There were times when my sympathies would have been with the Parks and Galleries Committee! Museum curators have their foibles and hobby-horses too. It is right and proper that they should have to make out a convincing case for an acquisition if it is going to be a costly one. The traditional British system of governance by amateurs has much to be said for it, always provided the amateurs are men and women of discrimination and well-informed in the field they are administering.

The efficiency of the trustee, and indeed of the committee system, is another matter. Boards and committees composed of busy public figures cannot be constantly in session, and meetings have to be fixed far in advance. This may serve for general administrative purposes, but is quite useless for dealing with purchases in the open market where speed of decision may be vital. In many museums the director must refer any purchase, or at any rate any purchase at more than a quite nominal figure, to his committee or trustees, and unless there is an arrangement whereby he can get a decision by telephoning the chairman or some member or members in whom responsibility has been vested, he will miss great opportunities. This has, in fact, happened all too often. The nation or the municipality have lost treasure after treasure which they might have had for a fraction of the price at which they subsequently changed hands. The person who knows most about such offers usually is the keeper of the department concerned, and the person who knows best whether the museum can afford to close with an offer is the director. The responsibility of committee or trustees surely is to satisfy themselves that the director is conforming to the general lines of policy periodically reviewed.

There was a time when trustees and committees met mainly to consider purchases. A museum which moves with the times has many other things to think of. This must have added much to the involvement of the governing bodies, and to the areas in which they can be of practical help. A local councillor who knows little about painting or natural history may know a great deal about building or education or finance, to say nothing of side-issues such as catering, things which occupy a far larger proportion of the director's attention than they could have done half-a-century ago. The most conservative trustee is aware that his museum or gallery is no longer merely a private collection writ large.

It is when we accept the suggestion that a museum, to be fully effective, may have to be more than an institution of learning, may in fact have to have an element of creative artistry in direction, that the relationship between director and governing body becomes rather delicate. If there is one thing a committee cannot do it is to create a work of art. It is perhaps a pretentious term to use about an exercise which involves merely careful planning, good taste and a dash of imagination; but so many people must contribute to the result that to develop the original idea into something new and exciting generates many of the tensions present in creating any work of art. The governing body should certainly approve the idea in the first place. Ecclesiastical conclaves no doubt approved the ideas for frescoes or windows in a medieval church, as Ludovico Moro may have approved the cartoon for Leonardo's 'Last Supper' which he commissioned; but how the idea is developed and executed is a process so personal that its ultimate success may well be endangered by interference and criticism.

What I am saying is that the creative process demands the pressure of a dominant urge, singleness of purpose, and that any concession or compromise is likely to weaken the result, even to nullify it. No one would seriously suggest that in the average museum or gallery this pitch of creative tension is happening all the time, certainly not on a major scale, but it is one of the happy aspects of the modern museum that more and more it does give opportunities for using people with creative zeal, and there must be areas where such people can have their head. The opportunity may be nothing more than a piece of presentation to be done with extreme sensitivity and good taste. It may be a daring discarding of convention turning the humdrum into something arresting and entrancing. Rarely, it may be a highly original and beautiful sequence of displays challenging enough to spark off a touch of genius. There are few enough opportunities for self-expression for the young men and women who pour out of our art colleges every year, and too many of them are driven into the dreary wilderness of mere self-assertion. It has been one of the pleasures of my later years in the museum profession to see some of these people find their niches, to the great profit of the museum. It would be a tragedy if the dead hand of uncomprehending authority should ever frustrate them.

The gap between professionals and amateurs in museums has so widened in recent years that it doubly underlines the problem of the governing body. The development in standards of curatorship, discussed elsewhere, has been promoted and organized by bodies such as the Museums Association and the International Council of Museums, and by a growing literature including serial publications such as *The Museums Journal* and *Museum*. Members of governing bodies may attend and speak at meetings of the Museums Association, and do so frequently, which has gone a long way to help some at least of the 'amateurs' to see problems from the same angle as the professionals. Yet it is not to be expected that the first, in their very much part-time capacity, will often acquire the expertise or instinctive judgement of the second. Few of them would dispute this. This must be specially true of a body whose members have other probably overriding responsibilities, for example councillors for whom the Parks and Galleries Committee is just another committee. Here, too, politics may cloud judgement. The museum professional may have to modify his arguments to enable them to have a chance in the hurly-burly of town-council polemics. Things are of course quite different in the trustee museums. Trustees, unless they are merely *ex officio*, are appointed for their interest in what the museum is all about, not infrequently they are men and women who are themselves distinguished authorities in one of the museum's fields. Yet in terms of pure museology the trustee is hardly more of a professional than the town councillor is, and in an age which tends to leave things more and more to the 'expert' it is not surprising if there is a tendency to re-assess the situation.

How, in general terms, might we change things for the better?

Governing bodies are composed of representatives of the community, whether elected or appointed for their special qualifications, and a primary responsibility must always be to safeguard collections which are the 'property' of the community. Even if they had no other reason for existence, such bodies are necessary to preserve the cultural heritage intact. This is something which cannot be left to the professionals. The professional by his very nature and training is biased towards one field or another, and every museum man knows how the emphasis shifts with staff changes and from one generation of curators to another. It is not implied that a director with *avant garde* views would dispose of a Rembrandt to strengthen his examples of the Ecole de Paris, but anyone who has been concerned with a disposals board knows that where second- or third-line material is being dealt with, things may get on to the disposals list which a future generation of curators will regret. Hence it is wise to have one or two trustees on the board, even if there are grumbles about their conservatism. I say trustees advisedly, for it must be obvious that an ordinary member of a Parks and Galleries Committee would be unlikely to possess the degree of connoisseurship to enable him to play an effective part in discussion of the merits of a work whose fate might be hanging in the balance. Trusteeship, in some form, seems to me the proper principle for the appointment of governing bodies, whether the museum be national, local authority, university or private foundation. But the method of election of trustees is vital. They must be independent of every sort of pressure, political or otherwise. The interest of the museum alone must be their yardstick, whatever outside policies may try to dictate. Here I must turn again to the experience of the United States, which has seen more successful developments in the museum field than any other country over the past century. The conclusion of Coleman is that the 'independent self-perpetuating board' of trustees offers the best safeguard.

Coleman here is particularly concerned with what we in this country would call municipal museums. When he wrote, there were only three public museums under city control in the United States, a form of management which, he says, 'does not have many advocates'. This does not mean the others were independent of municipal funds. It is, in fact, normal practice there for the museum to occupy a building owned by the city and to receive appropriations of money from the city, yet to remain independent. There is no likelihood of the building being withdrawn by the city, although there are many fluctuations or even withdrawals of the city's contribution to running costs, for example in times of economic pressures. The balance in such institutions is maintained through large private endowments coming from membership of museum societies, from wealthy patrons, even from industry, and careful diversification of income is the strength of great museums like the Metropolitan in New York, which is wealthier than the National Museum in Washington itself. In such places as the Metropolitan the trustees, as board of management, are in a very powerful position. It is however understood, I think, that they do not dictate to the museum: 'The trustee's duty', says Coleman, 'is to have the museum run, not to run it.' Yet this certainly does not mean he is a rubber stamp. He is deeply immersed in policy making, in appointing the right staff, in raising money; and in this last field the American museums are indeed fortunate, since their boards include some of the shrewdest financial brains in the country, from whom the museums receive free counsel. It is small wonder if some of the city museums in the United States can achieve what few other museums in the world can.

The term 'self-perpetuating trustees' must inevitably cause some raising of eyebrows on this side of the Atlantic. It will be argued that while this method of filling vacancies on the board may safeguard the museum from political interference, it is scarcely democratic and might not serve the interests of the community. Coleman himself remarks on the tendency for elderly trustees to be replaced by men of their own age, so that boards can lose youth and vigour and perpetuate a conservative attitude to the changing functions of museums. Perhaps the answer lies in the massive strengthening of supporting membership until this is so wide-based as to form an electorate to whom trustees are responsible. This would seem a logical step in the United States, where supporting membership is almost a *sine qua non* of any major museum, but in this country the movement is represented by 'friends of the museum' organizations which are still too tentative, too far from being broad-based enough to bear any sort of responsibility for museums and galleries. In the United States, bodies of members in return for their substantial financial contributions are made to feel they have a real stake in the museum, although often I think they are more a sort of privileged *cognoscenti* to whom the doors are sometimes opened after public closing-time so that they may enjoy the Titians in

116

tuxedos. Certainly they are not a cross-section of the community. The organization I have in mind must not be narrowly exclusive, not a sort of museum club which the average citizen would be shy of applying to join even if he could afford the subscription, but broad-based associations through which the public could identify themselves with particular institutions which interested them. Subscriptions would be nominal. The price of membership would be a real and continuing evidence of interest, and there would be opportunities for members to put forward their views either in writing or at meetings. The basic function of such associations would be a double one: the leavening of the wider community, focusing present responsibilities of all taxpayers and ratepayers to form an inner community whose interest in museums and galleries must be positive and articulate. Such an association, open to anyone to join, is entirely democratic, and its members would have the right to fill by voting at least a proportion of the seats at meetings of the governing body of their museum.

This proposal needs a great deal of thinking through, but I make it because in a long career I have so often been made aware of an immense fund of public good-will towards museums, and because I feel this could and should be put to work. I cannot say too often that public administration lags far behind the public itself in its attitude to museums. The democratic machine has been creaking for a long time. The answer does not lie in some extreme alternative system, as some are already beginning to murmur, but in applying oil to the machine in the right places, so that every smallest cog can exert its contribution; for we are apt to forget that in the democratic machine it is the small cogs which together must supply the drive, not the drive which must turn the cogs. The citizen, in fact, must do more than register his vote, whether in central or local government, or in a trade union. There must be means whereby he can have his say in addition to the ballot-box, means whereby he can make a positive contribution, however modest, in fields where his interests lie. It may be that the devolution of responsibility upon volunteer bodies of dedicated citizens such as I have advocated for museums may in fact be capable of wider application. The complexities of economic, industrial and political issues are such that far too much has to be done in the name of people who do not begin to understand those issues, and the result is a growing monopoly by professional and specialist advisers. The professional adviser is essential, but laymen capable of assessing his advice intelligently and so of forming judgements on it are equally essential.

Such a transfer of power to a trustee system, the trustees representing that part of the community which has elected to identify itself with the interests of museums and galleries, no doubt will seem an unnecessary complication to those who still believe in the capability of central and local government representatives fully to express the will of those they represent. To my mind, administration has become too intricate by far for any one set of ordinary men and women to cope with it in depth efficiently, and the new two-tier system of local government, with regional and district councils, can only add to the web of problems and responsibilities. Indeed, it may even add a new element of tension. Before the system had even got off the ground, it produced at least one exhibition of inter-tier jealousy in the cultural field in the shape of a tug-of-war over who was to run the Edinburgh International Festival—Edinburgh district, or the Lothians region! That was a dispute about possession of a prestige event. We simply do not know how less prestigious responsibilities like museums, about which neither public nor press has ever been particularly vigilant, will fare under the new system. It is not enough for citizens genuinely interested to buttonhole a councillor and trust that what they urge him to say will be said with equal force at a forthcoming meeting of council, or if it will be said at all.

But mention of the Edinburgh Festival brings to mind a working example of something like the sort of trustee system I have suggested. Up to now, the Council of the Festival has been formed partly of town councillors and partly of representatives of the Festival Society, the *ex officio* chairman being the Lord Provost of the city; and behind the Council is a programme panel of people with specialist knowledge both initiating ideas and supplying criticism. The Society elects its representatives to the Council at its annual general meeting. It is a private society, self-perpetuating in that its members join by invitation. The museum society which I have advocated, and which would elect its quota of trustees to the museum board, would be a public

118

body, virtually open to anyone willing to stand up and be counted as one committed to supporting the museum and furthering its cause. If witness is an element essential to keeping alive churches, it could also have a part to play in keeping democracy alive.

XIII *The Museum Image*

IN 1971 THE Bow Group published a pamphlet on a national policy for museums and galleries under the title *Dusty Heritage*. The pamphlet contains many suggestions worth consideration, but perhaps the most significant thing about it is the title. One must of course make allowances for the need to choose a title which would make an impact; but anyone familiar with museums as they are today, still more with their plans and aspirations, knows how utterly inappropriate it is. Certainly it would have applied fifty years ago, but now even the least progressive museums, with a few exceptions, do not treat their collections as lumber in an attic. I am sure the author was well aware of this. He shows himself sufficiently informed of some at least of the progress in museums for it to be otherwise. If however his meaning is that it is the image of museums in the minds of some of our administrators which is dusty then he is well justified, and this image is perpetuated every time some public figure in a speech uses the word museum as synonymous with scrapheap. More than anything else, what museums need is a campaign to show them as they really are.

The public relations officer possibly has been as difficult to introduce into museums as the display officer. Academic staff in time usually come to appreciate the efforts of a skilled display man to show their material to best effect, but they are very suspicious where 'selling' their wares to the man in the street is concerned. Their aversion is understandable. Anyone who has conducted a press view of a major art exhibition will remember the glazed look in the eyes of reporters from the popular papers, and the inevitable final question put with the first spark of interest: how much is it all insured for? One is left with the anxious hope that the public will see more in it than those young men and women conditioned to react only to the crudely sensational. The public almost invariably does. That at least is my experience.

The public is not altogether the indifferent, dull-witted congrega-
tion of sensation-seekers which the popular media believe it to
be—and which, at the other extreme, some of my late colleagues
in museums also believe it to be. Of course there are millions of
people whose tastes are so far deadened by what the media offer
that it is hard to get through to them—Boyle's Law applies here
as in so much else—but there are also millions who are almost
pathetically eager to learn about other lands and other cultures,
other ages, or indeed the things of their own age and culture if
put to them in a new light and in language they can understand. I
have seen the museum cinema filled and filled again on a winter's
night by people wanting to see 'educational' films—travel, art,
nature, technology and science—which no commerical cinema
today would have touched. Such films offer precisely what the
museum itself offers, but in the familiar cinema environment.
The existing popularity of museums—and the statistics proving
this themselves need to be hammered home—is capable of massive expansion and needs only persistent publicity about what to
see and where to see it.

Public relations is an accepted practice in most museums today,
whether conducted by a special department as at the Victoria and
Albert or only by a member of staff with this additional responsibility. Over the past ten or fifteen years there has been a steady
improvement in the standard of public relations work, and the
quality of posters and publications has been exemplary and has
itself been a contribution to the education of public taste in the
printer's art. Where the more discriminating public is concerned,
this kind of publicity, so far as it goes, is on the right lines,
because more vulgar and aggressive methods of advertising
would be totally wrong for institutions which are trying to raise
cultural standards. The only trouble with the output of posters is
that there is not nearly enough of it. Advertising, in the world in
general, has the opposite fault. It is big business, so big that it
has polluted our culture, thrusting itself into our townscapes and
landscapes, consuming newsprint which should be available for
straight news, informed comment and other features of journals
in the past, and destroying those powers of discrimination which
are aids to the process of natural selection and ultimately of
human progress. In the face of this avalanche of importunity, the
discreet measures which museums have been able to take to keep

themselves in the public eye have no impact on mass audiences. The man or woman conditioned by commercial advertising—and in some degreee we are all affected—is not likely to be drawn to venture into a museum for the first time by the discreet announcements now issued by our museums. Yet that first time is of vital importance. We must get through to the unconverted. The essentials of popular advertising for museums therefore are two: in the first place to bring about that 'first time', in the second to make sure that the newcomer likes what he finds and comes back for more. The second requirement has become much less of a problem than it was. The new look which more and more museums are striving to give to their entrance halls and primary galleries is an eye-opener to many people still labouring under popular misconceptions about museums. But we have to go much further. We have to make absolutely certain that the first impact kills the outmoded image for ever, and this is a job which the public relations officer has to urge upon the director and his display staff if they are not already aware of it. The other essential, to bring about that 'first time', is a real challenge to the public relations man who, knowing what it takes to arrest public attention, must also have a shrewd eye for what the museum has or might have possessing the necessary appeal. Dramatic content, topicality, sheer beauty—all those things might count. But the appeal must be in depth, hinting at much more to come. It is a task which calls for great gifts.

Public relations is of course a two-way operation. It involves not only publicizing a product or a service but also feeding back information about what the community wants. This is just as true of museum public relations work, but one also has to take into account the element of resistance which, as I have already indicated, may be present in the museum itself. It is a devious sort of resistance, ranging from disapproval of what some staff regard as vulgar advertising to the suspicion of some specialists who are themselves contributors to the media and who consider —often justifiably—that they themselves are best able to publicize what is going on in their department. Discretion is needed in the second case. Such specialists are authorities and whatever they write is *ex cathedra*. Some of them are even household names. It would be unthinkable to interfere with such activities. On the other hand, not many authoritative writers of this kind can add massively to the numbers of the general public coming to the museum, and this is the main target of the public relations officer. As to sheer conservative resistance to any sort of publicity, powers of diplomacy are one of the prerequisites of anyone entering museum public relations, and here I think it is important that he or she should be a person of some scholarly background or at least should have much real sympathy towards the scholar's attitude and be able to talk in such terms as will reassure him, otherwise he may find himself in a very difficult position indeed. Establishing a feed-back of public opinion to the museum is of high importance. There are various ways of doing this. One may take an opinion poll from visitors, a method much favoured in the United States and quite often practised here also. My own view on this method is that, while it can produce interesting comment and sometimes valuable ideas, if it became regular practice it would give visitors the impression they were under observation and might annoy and alienate certain people. Also I have some reservations on the validity of replies to pollsters, especially when such replies have to be fitted into the categories of a questionnaire. It is really more important to tap the views of people beyond the walls of the museum. I do not suggest stopping people in the street, but much more use could be made of the many invitations which come to museums to send someone to address societies, schools and clubs. There is no great enthusiasm, as a rule, to respond to such invitations. Too often they are passed to junior members of staff, so that the literary society of, say, Puddlecombe-in-the-Marsh finds itself addressed on some such likely subject as 'Red Figure Attic Vases' or 'The Coleoptera of the Iberian Peninsula', with predictable results. It is an opportunity wasted. In my experience, if the speaker is at all persuasive audiences will generally take half-an-hour or even more on learning how someone else earns his living, and if the audience is given an opportunity to ask questions and voice its views it will end by getting really interested in the problems of museums. Obviously this depends a good deal on the nearness of one or two good museums; but in towns and cities it should be possible to establish a two-way traffic of ideas which could bring the community and its museums into a new relationship.

American museums have a long start in the use of radio and television for spreading the image of the museum. Some of them have had regular radio programmes on the air since the thirties.

Coleman stresses the importance of professionalism in such programmes. He seems rather to question the educational value of
this kind of activity, referring to it as 'attenuated museum work',
but there can be no doubt of the usefulness as a public relations
exercise of constantly bringing the museum into the home. The
multiplicity of stations in the United States vastly increases the
scope, and the spread of local radio in Britain may offer similar
opportunities here. So far, the B.B.C. and I.T.V. have not
seriously attempted to exploit museums, which they seem to
regard as property-rooms from which to draw material for programmes fitting into their own patterns. Indeed it is one of their
weaknesses that unless an idea fits neatly into the established
patterns of producers and commentators there is small likelihood
it will be taken up. To project the New Museum on the screens of
Britain, therefore, demands a considerable break-through. In
saying this I am not wholly blaming the broadcasting authorities.
I think museums should be diligently exploring the possibilities,
not on their own but, bearing Coleman's advice about professionalism in mind, in conjunction with some of the more imaginative
producers.

Publications are perhaps not thought of normally as part of the
process of projecting the museum, yet they form an important
element of its impact. Some publications—I am thinking more
especially of expensive, specialist monographs in very limited
editions—may seem to have little to do with public relations, but
they are links with scholars all over the world and also with other
museums, as there is a wide-ranging system of mutual exchange.
They are therefore vehicles whereby the museum's scholarly repute is carried abroad. If scholarly repute scarcely seems to be
part of public relations, it has to be remembered that the museum
is not an expendable commodity which is being advertised, but a
heritage for which a sense of public pride is to be fostered, and its
international status is something to be kept before the public. The
format of those monographs and serials may not be important to
their scholarly readers, but it is important as a status symbol in
the best sense to those jealous of the museum's image, as those
publications will lie on the bookstalls of the issuing museum and
of many other museums as well, so that one may look on them as
envoys not only within the world of scholarship but to thousands
who will do no more than browse. At the other extreme it can

hardly be necessary to emphasize the popular impact of ephemera ranging from handouts and lay-out plans to lavishly-illustrated picture books and children's publications. They have an enormous distribution and must make an appropriate appeal to the eye. At the same time they should be models of fine production, in everything from typeface to style. Standards are already high, nowhere more than in some H.M.S.O. productions. The use of regular bulletins to publicize new activities has a long way to go in this country. A consistent high standard is possible only if large numbers of the public can be induced to subscribe or if there is a massive subsidy, and subsidy through advertisement pages also depends on a large public. Bulletins seem to flourish, relatively so at least, in the United States, where the museum membership system guarantees a fairly high minimum distribution, enabling the editor to know where he stands. The *Scottish Art Review*, an organ of the Glasgow Art Gallery and Museums Association, is one of the few well-produced magazines of the kind to have survived successfully in Britain, and it has done so only by very careful business management and the exploration of all avenues of subsidy from direct grants to the subsequent use of colour-blocks for picture postcards. As a public relations exercise such magazines are wasted effort unless they give the impression of reflecting a flourishing enterprize.

Mention of postcards directs us to one of the most important publicity activities open to the museum. The public itself will happily subsidize it, particularly if the museum is large enough to support a wide range of postcards on its bookstalls. Timidity here spells failure. A booth with half-a-dozen cards on it attracts no attention, while a stall with forty or fifty issues creates a lively market place. First-rate colour work is of course essential, because the public is now conditioned to colour-reproductions which are both excellent and cheap. Here the advice of public relations staff is of first importance in choice of subject, because too often the specialist has little notion about what appeals to the average citizen, still less about what will take the eye of his small son or daughter, who form a high proportion of the consumers in this branch of publicity.

At the core of any publicity policy for museums should surely be the urgent need to invest with a living, warm aura an institution which, almost by definition, has for so long been regarded as a tomb of dead cultures. A power-station is not a fossil because it draws its energy from the fossil products of the Carboniferous age. A museum is, or should be, generating present benefits for the community from the debris of the past, and one should no more develop its publicity solely on the basis of advertising inert items in its collections than one would classify a power-station as a coal-storage depot. It is the positive function of the museum which needs to be hammered home ceaselessly, by poster, publications, radio programmes and all other means. But no publicity channel is more important than the personality of the public relations officer himself. If he has a way with him—and this does not mean turning himself into a department-store Santa Claus!— he will do more than any expensive campaign to make the community aware of the museum as a place not merely where certain things are but where certain things happen. This, basically, is the image which he has to create. He must meet as many people as he can and meet them often: through business clubs and professional bodies, schools and universities, women's associations, industry. There is something for all of these in the museum. If there is not, there should be. And here again we return to the question of feed-back, because it cannot be emphasized too often that if the public relations officer discovers there is a section of the community to which he has nothing to offer he must do what he can to change this.

Press coverage is a subject in itself. Here again the United States has a big lead. Even before the war, in a typical winter month the *New York Times* carried twenty-five columns of stories about museum activities. In this country the situation has deteriorated. In pre-war days I do not recall having too much difficulty in getting half-a-column or even more on some worth-while museum event into one of the morning papers where now a mention would be looked on as generous treatment, and in my experience so far as museums are concerned the 'nationals' are interested only in what might be called disaster material, which could be anything from a major break-in to—an actual instance!—persistent high mortality in an ornamental goldfish pond. A real problem, of course, is the drastic reduction in size of British papers today, partly due to the chronic newsprint shortage, together with the increasingly high proportion of space devoted to commercial advertising; while again British dailies, by comparison with American, pay relatively small attention to local news. Probably the best method now of obtaining coverage is through the press-conference, which normally is quite well attended provided it is linked to an event with potential news value, such as a major temporary exhibition or an important (and valuable!) acquisition. This gives the press a wide-open chance to get their own angle on the news, which may be straight reportage, gossip-column material, or merely a picture. It also helps to build up closer relations between museum staff and particular reporters or critics, so that eventually papers get the habit of telephoning on chance if they happen to have space to fill.

The main index of success or failure in public relations is and always will be attendance figures. Some museum authorities have affected indifference to attendance figures, maintaining it is quality rather than quantity which is important. Too often this attitude, I suspect, is a cover-up for poor results. Profitability in a museum truly enough is reflected in many things which cannot be measured, particularly sevices to scholarship and to education, but public response is an important item on the credit side in ways quite other than the reduction of *per capita* cost. Critics of the attendance figure index point to the fact that a rainy summer or a wild winter will push up or lower numbers without any real meaning in terms of benefits received by the community. I have never accepted this. I have known too many cases of people who came in out of the rain and stayed, and returned another day, and got the habit, because they were at first surprised then interested by what they found. The 'quality' attendance will always be maintained, because it is comprised of people who are interested anyway. It is the mass attendance which indicates whether the museum is breaking through the crust of indifference. The museum has much to offer, but unless large numbers are some-how persuaded to come in the offer in the main will go a-begging because no one knows about it. There will always be those who come in only for shelter, the down-and-outs who have nowhere to go for warmth, but even they are not wholly unresponsive and who knows what comforts they do not find beyond warmth and a bench to sit on? It would be an austere and chilly administration which did not count them into the credit figures. But the most signal justification for relying on the index of attendance figures may be seen in the graph for the whole country over a period.

There were very high figures towards the end of the nineteenth century, when movements for self-improvement and adult education directed people to any institution where they could acquire knowledge free. Across the disturbed years from the First to the Second World War the graph is uncertain and frequently drops. Since 1945 there has been an upward trend in figures for the museums and galleries of the United Kingdom, a trend which rises steadily across the board. It is not due to any change in the weather pattern. It means only one thing: that museums are increasingly popular. In part this is due to modernization programmes, but it is due also to the better image being put about, in fact to better public relations.

XIV *Ringing the Changes*

Dr Parr in 1962 expressed some impatience with advocates of constant change in museums. He maintained it betokened a chase after popularity rather than devotion to education, as the basic laws of science, the ultimate values, are unchanging. But as he goes on to admit, even the eternal verities have to be clothed anew for each successive generation.

The need for regular changes in presentation exists in every museum open to the public, and the smaller the museum the greater the need. There are of course fixed stars which are part of the very firmament. It would be unthinkable if the Rosetta Stone were not perpetually in display at the British Museum, or the Venus of Milo in the Louvre. But as I have consistently stressed, nothing does more harm to the museum than to give an impression that nothing ever happens there, and so maximum variation of presentation commensurate with the main functions of the museum—research and education—must always be kept in mind. Dr Parr's warning about change is not to be disregarded. Certainly the museum should not be a weather-cock turning to record every shift of fashion in the gimmickry of window-dressing. Indeed it has a duty to be discriminating in its responses to popular demand. The fact remains that communication is a science—or an art—which must be infinitely flexible and responsive to altering viewpoints and idioms, and if a museum neglects this it has only itself to blame if it finds it has lost touch with the community it serves. No doubt it will lag a little, as any large institution must do; but this lag is far more serious now than it was in more leisured times, and the 'mausoleum' spectre is far closer to our heels in these days of instant information than it was when nobody expected a museum to be anything but static.

On a modest scale, museums have been making concessions to this need for change for a long time. Features such as the 'exhibit of the month' have been experimented with for as long as I can remember. These exhibits usually take some such form as a case near the entrance spotlighting an object of particular interest, perhaps with a topical connotation, and probably with its special significance more fully described than it would be on the label in a permanent gallery. But exhibits of this sort really do no more than pay lip-service to the need to keep abreast of the times. On a larger scale, the gallery or court of recent acquisitions is another fairly common feature drawing attention to what is new, fairly common that is in great museums such as the Victoria and Albert; but it hardly fulfils the need for change, as few museums are fortunate enough to be able to modify such a display substantially more than once or twice in a year.

There is a type of permanent exhibit with what might be called a built-in capacity for change, and indeed on occasion for making news itself. Science museums rather monopolize this small field. An obvious example of what I mean is the weather-recording apparatus owned by many museums but often relegated to an obscure corner, the apparatus of barographs and rain-gauges and wind-recorders usually retained primarily to illustrate how such scientific work is carried out. With the help of an ingenious display-specialist this can very easily be re-deployed to provide a sort of public weather-station where everyone—and Britain is notoriously a weather-conscious nation!—can see precisely what the situation is in the area day-by-day and at the same time learn the principles and language of weather-recording. This is particularly valuable in an urban civilization such as ours, where the signs and portents which are second-nature to an old countryman have long passed even from the racial memory except for the odd tag about a red sky in the morning. If this seems slightly frivolous, I can only say that even as things are, there are individuals who, before committing themselves to some outdoor enterprize, go out of their way to inspect the museum apparatus as though it were invested with some special authority which their own domestic barometers did not possess! Then—and this can be a news-making exhibit with considerable impact—there is the seismograph. A large and sensitive seismograph fully installed and operative will bring telephone inquiries from the press and visits from their photographers every time there are rumours of earthquakes anywhere from Persia to Peru, and if the installation can be arranged to indicate direction the museum may be of real service, certainly to the media. If this gives the impression that in striving to keep museums in the forefront of events I would have them in league with sensation-hungry reporters, more concerned with scoops than with the human suffering which may lie behind the news, I can only say this sort of service may bring people far nearer to the stricken community, and more swiftly generate sympathy. The dramatic lurches of the needle on the carboned surface of the recording drum have a stark immediacy. And if the seismographs are supplemented by sound recordings of earthquakes such as are available at certain observatories, there is no better demonstration of how a museum can awaken people to the realities of the world they live in.

A more ambitious feature in the same category is the planetarium. Both on the Continent and in America planetaria are accepted as natural accompaniments to science museums, but in the United Kingdom there is a certain reluctance to introduce them, partly no doubt because of the high capital cost of installation. Yet in this age they are essential educational tools, and they fulfil admirably the need for an element of constant change in the museum. There is an impression here, I think, that planetaria are principally a spectacular means of learning the basic facts of astronomy, and that they belong either with observatories or nautical schools on the one hand, or on the other with the entertainment industry—this latter because Madame Tussaud's was the first place to instal one, at least on a large scale. Both the Deutsches Museum and the American Museum of Natural History long ago proved them to be essential complements to the telescopes, astrolabes and other instruments of the kind for which museums are now willing to offer inflated, art market prices, but which in themselves have little meaning for the layman unless the dimensions they open up to the specialist can be opened up for him too. In recent years the German and Japanese optical industries have competed in the production of more and more ingenious planetaria, and variations in the programmes which can be mounted are almost infinite. Space exploration has lent an added incentive. Planetaria provide the means to illustrate moon and planet probes in the simplest terms, and with a sense of the actual to bring statistics alive. And on an everyday plane, modifications of the instruments allow the theatre to become also a climaterium, where the principles of weather can be illustrated and the formation and behaviour of clouds demonstrated.

I have already discussed at some length (in Chapter V, 'Taking Museums Seriously') how museums can and should do something to interpret advances in industrial and other fields. It is unnecessary to go over this ground again; but obviously there is no better way of maintaining an element of change in the museum than to provide this sort of gloss on the contemporary scene. It may range from comparisons from various methods of constructing a Channel tunnel or of building oil-rig platforms to marshalling the pros and cons of issues between developers and conservationalists—for example if a new airfield threatened natural resources or amenities. Such activities might be relatively costly, both in money and in time spent on them, but often the bodies concerned would not be averse to providing both and would look upon it as a public relations exercise.

As to the main collections in the public galleries of a museum, no one will seriously suggest those be subject to frequent radical change. However, it is a good thing that the old practice of issuing detailed guide-books has gone, guide-books which recorded precisely which objects were where on the shelves of each individual case, because this degree of inflexibility is acceptable neither to the specialist nor to the layman. There must always be room for change and growth. But quite apart from the physical and logistical problems of trying to move them, the main collections must preserve a basic stability in their lay-out in the interests of everyone seriously trying to use the museum. Improvements in methods of presentation must change them in time, but this is a slow process.

The main opportunity for ringing the changes lies in the temporary exhibition. This is the vehicle for underlining new discoveries or for throwing new light on old discoveries, for imaginative interpretation, for bringing together related treasures from many sources. A necessarily brief duration concentrates public interest. Temporary exhibitions of course have been mounted in museums for a long time, but incorporating them as a constant and regular feature of the museum year is an activity which has expanded in fairly recent times, and the pace of expansion has accelerated since the war. Factors which may have helped to stimulate this as far as Great Britain is concerned are the great Royal Academy loan exhibitions of the thirties and after, the big Government-sponsored displays of the immediate post-war years, and the Edinburgh International Festival. I was myself involved in one of the first group, in two of the second and in a high proportion of the third, and came to the conclusion very early, as did many of my colleagues, that museums had barely begun to exploit opportunities offered by the temporary exhibition. It is a different story in museums now. Even so, few among our major museums, far less the smaller institutions, are yet equipped adequately to mount more than a very occasional first-class temporary exhibition.

More than once it has been suggested here that the museum, in certain aspects, should be a work of art in its own right. This is particularly true in the case of the temporary exhibition. Although years of scholarship and effort and a substantial sum of money may be behind it, the exhibition may last no more than two or three weeks. Its success depends upon its being instantly articulate, persuasive and absorbing. It must be a memorable experience—all too soon it will be nothing but a memory. The tempo must be exciting. A man or woman of good taste should be able to arrange the display in a permanent gallery to most people's satisfaction, but it needs something of a maestro to get the best out of a temporary exhibition. It cannot be done with a sheaf of statistics and a blueprint alone, any more than the score alone can determine the performance of a symphony. In fact the temporary exhibition is not primarily an exercise for the benefit of scholars and specialists, who have probably seen most of the material on show anyway. Essentially it is for the public, although a discriminating public, and is an invitation to share an experience which may add a new dimension to their pleasure as well as to their knowledge. I well remember my first real introduction to Chinese art in a lecture by Lawrence Binyon, as I recall being personally initiated into aspects of Japanese art by Adrian Koop at the Victoria and Albert. Binyon, of course, was a poet, but Koop with his gentle enthusiasm and his verse-mnemonics was an artist too in his way, and it is this sort of interpretation which so many temporary exhibitions demand but do not always get.

Some doubts and criticisms have been growing, and it is right to review them. Critics have claimed that the more ambitious type of temporary exhibition is no longer practicable. For one thing, there has been a decline of the public appetite which the cultural short-commons of the war years brought about. For another, foreign galleries are less willing to lend, and the same is true of private owners: there are too many organized robberies, and a crazy inflationary economy has raised insurance values until masterpieces have been placed beyond a borrower's reach. There are, in fact plenty of good excuses for doing nothing, or as little as possible. But the excuses will satisfy only those who are looking for them. All that has happened is that the traditional, if admittedly often splendid displays of celebrated 'old masters' or of so-and-so's collection of Impressionists or Post-Impressionists have become much more difficult to get, and instead of them we must rely upon theme-based exhibitions which do not depend to the same degree on large numbers of excessively valuable works. There have been many such exhibitions in recent years both in London and the provinces: one thinks perhaps especially of some brilliant examples at the National Portrait Gallery. My own museum was fortunate in being able to mount several, usually in conjunction with the Edinburgh Festival, some of them later transferred to London, either at the Victoria and Albert Museum or the South Bank. 'Byzantine Art' in 1958 certainly leaned heavily upon valuable material drawn from both sides of the Iron Curtain. On the other hand, 'Indian Art and the Dance', with its listening-booths for the music of sitars and other instruments, and its evening demonstrations by one of India's leading dancers, showed how relatively few costly loans may by means of carefully devised links add up to an exhibition just as entrancing in its way. One of the most remarkable of such thematic exhibitions was that extraordinary pageant of treasures of the City Livery Companies of London entitled 'Pomp', sent to Edinburgh in 1969 by the Worshipful Company of Goldsmiths as a tribute to the Festival. Exhibitions of this kind depend much less on the works of art involved than on the knowledge, enthusiasm and ingenuity of those who devise them.

Heavy cost is always a major argument in the case against regular temporary exhibitions. The biggest item on the debit side of any exhibition involving large-scale borrowing is insurance premiums. National museums for a considerable time past have been able to escape expenditure on insurance by invoking a Government indemnity scheme, and this has now been extended to cover exhibitions sponsored by the Arts Councils. It seems reasonable to press for a further extension of this scheme or principle to the local or regional authorities so as to relieve at least the major museums of the country of a nearly insuperable bar to enterprize in the exhibition field. Another heavy cost element, and one which could be even heavier for thematic exhibitions, is the hidden cost of staff time and effort, to say nothing of special material and equipment and in certain cases the fees of outside contractors. Outlay on special material and equipment will be very much eased, if not eliminated, by the provision of a gallery or hall designed solely for temporary displays—virtually a blank area with a completely flexible system of lighting, rather like a television or film studio. With it will be built up a suite of 'props', including cases capable of being dismantled for storage. Such a fully-equipped gallery does away with the considerable unseen cost in manpower-time of having to clear a permanent gallery for a temporary show. Staff time and effort have always to be paid for in terms of routine work left undone, but many big exhibitions today are not only funded but at least partly mounted by outside bodies. The Arts Councils are the most prominent example of this. Every museum has its special benefactors in respect of outside sponsors: I have already mentioned the Goldsmiths' Company. On occasions almost the entire responsibility is carried by an individual foreign museum, or indeed by a foreign government. Notable recent examples of such government sponsorship have been the Tutankhamun and Chinese art exhibitions in London. The impact of such lavish displays of major works upon the public imagination can be enormous; but without a careful follow-up they are fleeting, and there has been a good deal of justifiable uneasiness among responsible curators over the principle of risking masterpieces for ends which are purely political. It is quite another matter when an individual museum decides to design and lend abroad a thematic exhibition incorporating first-rate if not irreplaceable pieces. I recall such examples as 'Norwegian Art Treasures', shown both in Edinburgh and in London, and 'Scots in Sweden', involving years of research fortunately preserved in a catalogue still to be found years later on the bookstall in Nordiska Museet in Stockholm.

The pace of progress in science and technology means constant change is obligatory in any museum covering those fields, and the need for exhibitions here could bring intolerable pressure on staffs which increase slowly. Popular response to initiative by museums in attempting to cover the more dramatic advances, has usually been swift, as when moon-dust and moon-rock samples were placed on view following the landings. Several museums took the chance to back up the samples, not in themselves very enthralling visually, with demonstrations of how they were obtained and of their significance. An impact possibly even greater was made by early showings of the Mercury Space Capsule, still with the scorch-marks caused by its re-entry into the earth's atmosphere. N.A.S.A. was quick to co-operate with the Smithsonian, and subsequently showed its awareness of how museums could interpret its achievements by making the Capsule available in Britain and on the Continent. This sort of co-operation was much more than a routine exercise. When I suggested that the presence of an astronaut would enhance the occasion it resulted in a visit by Colonel John Glenn, and a follow-up staff visit to N.A.S.A. headquarters at Houston, Texas, produced material which enabled the museum to devise a permanent 'space' gallery complete with models of capsules and rockets as well as astronauts' equipment. This kind of liaison transforms a museum's attitude, and the attitude of the public towards it. There are authorities and industries in this country also no less ready to co-operate—even if the front door is not always the best avenue of approach!—but a good deal of missionary work still has to be done to persuade them actually to mount temporary exhibitions as distinct from supplying the museum with the means to mount its own.

Finally, where change is concerned, there is the face which the museum presents to the public, change in what may be called outward expression. Museums which seem to be quite aware of the need to present their collections in a new way and to modernize their decor are sometimes curiously immobile when it comes to what first meets the eye. Their entrance precinct is static, sphinx-like. It tends, of course, to be dominated by Doric columns or other features heavily committed to nineteenth-century solemnity and stability, but here a special effort has to be made to introduce animation. Even on the exterior of the building there are ways of modifying and multiplying notice-boards, for instance, without vulgarizing the frontage. They should always be brightly illuminated like shop-windows, even after closing-time; nor should posters and notices exhibited in them be left there until streaks of damp or condensation turn them into anti-notices. Expensive though it be, they should be renewed all the time, and everything must be done to keep changing the designs even if a poster is drawing attention to a permanent feature—it implies that *someone* is looking on it with a fresh eye. It might be mentioned here in passing that costs may be reduced a little by selling posters, for there is quite a good market for such things. Lighting, again, can be an important factor in altering the outward expression of the building.

As to the entrance area immediately within the doors, it is not difficult to plan this for maximum flexibility. Inquiry desks and publications kiosks do not have to be constantly moved around, but they should be re-dressed at intervals. The need from the sales point of view to mass publications and postcards has been mentioned in another place, but they should be re-shuffled too in changing patterns. Kiosks should be more like commercial bookshops and include outside publications among their wares, provided they are relevant: a quite normal practice in museums in the United States, and one which adds to the sense of move-ment. I realize there are trade difficulties in this country, com-petition with shops which have heavy overheads; but the present practice apart from anything else is prejudicial to the educational aims of the museum. The reproduction shop comes into the same category as the publications kiosk. It should always be included in the entrance precinct, not merely for the sake of sales, but because it adds to the air of the museum being 'in business' and also because it provides another area for changing decorative displays. And there is an amenity which belongs especially to this area and is much too timidly exploited in Britain: the use of living flowers and plants, which by their nature emphasize change. The effect on a visitor's receptivity of specimen pots and vases filled with fresh-cut flowers, and the drifts of perfume from them, which one finds in a place like Winterthur, has to be experienced to be believed. Fresh flowers would be costly if extended to the galleries in general, but quite attainable if confined to the entrance precinct, particularly if the museum is in a position to maintain its own greenhouse. Arrangement is as important as the blooms themselves. It is of course a subtle art in its own right; but it may be taken further and help to emphasize the changing seasons, either in the more obvious Western way or through cycles of symbolic displays as practised in China and Japan.

XV *Museums, Galleries and Stately Homes*

THE DIVIDING line between museums and galleries is more marked in some countries than in others, and in certain places it is blurred. Broadly speaking, however, galleries are the buildings where one goes to look at paintings, and perhaps at sculpture, while museums house everything else. Some galleries exhibit a few pieces of decorative art. Some museums have an anomalous enclave of paintings, as for example the Victoria and Albert, or perhaps of oriental paintings, which tend to be regarded as something exotic. Many of the world's greatest art institutes, from the Hermitage to the Metropolitan, are museums and galleries combined. But the dividing line between the fine arts and the rest is usually there, just the same—the fine arts are one thing, and the decorative arts quite something else.

I wonder if anything has done more to foster the popular misunderstanding about art than this incomprehensible belief, which amounts to a kind of class distinction. Not only has it perpetuated popular misunderstanding, but it has also encouraged an academic isolationism which begins in the universities and other teaching institutes and deprives hundreds of scholars of a breadth of view and interest which could only enhance their scholarship. Ultimate justification for the division, I would almost call it divorce, no doubt lies in the aims of the practitioners concerned, which in the case of the painters and sculptors seek the heights of human aspiration. These last, indeed, for three centuries or so have been free progressively more and more to indulge their capacity for self-expression, free to paint or sculpt as the spirit moved them, since—portraiture apart—they have not normally been required by society to conform to any precise function. Those who have practised what used to be called the applied arts, on the other hand, performed a practical service like any other tradesmen, and the Chippendales and the Lameries, even the man who wove the Apocalypse tapestries at Angers, by most critics have not been accepted as artists in the same sense as Rubens or Goya or Michelangelo.

There is much substance in the argument for this view. A truly great painting is a more important human document than the best effort of the best of cabinet-makers or silversmiths. But the great painting is a constituent part of the apex of a pyramid broad-based upon all the arts, its foundations the very stuff of craftsmanship, and without what lies below, the glorious apex would never have been reared. There is no dividing line between top and bottom in this pyramid. The category of the fine arts contains a high proportion of works which, however interesting they be to connoisseurs, however excellent in craftsmanship, are pedestrian efforts. The category of the decorative arts contains a vast number of works which either are masterpieces in themselves or in association with other things eloquently express the mood of an age. To make a hard and fast division between the two categories is an affront to both. At this time of new thinking about museums it is to be hoped long and deep thought will be given to this, and that our planning will not be prejudiced by basing it on old if time-honoured errors of judgement.

Occasionally museums do commission a work of art and place it on exhibition, but most art, both past and present, has been created to be seen and enjoyed in the context of the community the artist belongs to, or of some section of that community. Isolate it from its environment and its significance is apt to drain away from it, even if we are still able to admire it after a fashion. It becomes like a butterfly in an entomologist's cabinet, a specimen, but only the knowledgeable can re-create the scene of which it formed a part and in so doing give it some semblance of life. Set out in the drawer and labelled with others of its kind, its interest becomes merely clinical. That great connoisseur Sir Robert Witt began one of his books thus: 'Among the most pathetic figures in the world must be counted the men and women who may be seen slowly circumambulating the four walls with eyes fixed upon catalogue or guide-book, only looking up at intervals to insure that they are standing before the right picture.' When one thinks of it, surely it is a barbarous practice to hang rows of paintings on the walls of a gallery as if they were insects in an entomological cabinet. They have exactly the same dead, clinical look. Conditions have changed, of course. The monstrous overcrowding which forty years ago made one wilt and yawn in places like the Alte Pinacothek in Munich or the Accademia in Venice has given way to selectivity and elegance and to carefully grouped hanging indicating that the promoters recognize that too many paintings all together at once are a bore and cancel one another out. For me, the only difference from the old days is that the paintings now look a little embarrassed, and deprived. They were created by men for the joy and edification of men; but there, with the advantage of perfect air-conditioning and under lighting filtered of all harmful rays, they are condemned safely to survive for ever to be stared at by generations which can never quite feel at home with them. To make a new comparison, they are like fish out of water on a beautiful marble slab. Only in a few galleries such as the Phillips in Washington, former home of the collector himself and retaining a feeling of personality and intimacy, is there freedom from such frigidity. The extraordinary thing is that, for all the new thinking about museums, in our major galleries it seems to have occurred to no one that to hang paintings without even a word of explanation, without a general label outlining the scope of a school or the background of the pictures in a particular room, is virtually to exclude them from the full enjoyment of all but a few. Some years ago a *Burlington Magazine* editorial criticized this shortcoming trenchantly: it made 'tentative lovers of art . . . that bit more depressed, that bit more prepared to believe it another piece of upper-class mumbo-jumbo.' After all, as the writer pointed out, concert programmes are informative about the pieces to be played.

Museums of the decorative arts used to be every bit as remote. Ranks of silver tankards on glass shelves, rows of chairs protected from weary visitors by cords stretched between the arms, Greek vases stacked behind a barrier of wire netting, no less, in one pre-war German museum—fortunately I have forgotten which . . . No doubt it was the very obvious dreariness of such displays which forced curators quite a long time ago to begin to do something about it, and it was seen that a transformation could be wrought simply by bringing categories of materials such as metalwork, wood-carvings, ivories, ceramics, textiles, back into natural relationships with each other and grouping them together to illustrate styles or periods. Most museum men would agree that the effect of such grouping on the lay public has been considerable.

Study collections which formerly had shrivelled the interest of the layman were re-formed so that they were seen to be human documents, beauty which had been lost in the overcrowding and regimentation emerged again and took on its proper significance by association, as for example when copes and chasubles were grouped with chalices, pyxes and ciboria of their own time. The ultimate in this type of presentation, unfortunately far beyond the means of most museums, is The Cloisters in New York, where the rich store of medieval material in the Metropolitan was brought together with portions of old structures transported from European sites and re-erected in a building on the lines of an Italian abbey complete with campanile in a commanding position looking across the Sound to the Palisades.

No one who has seen this principle of reconstituting the art of the past in appropriate settings carried out lavishly and imaginatively will doubt that it should be extended to all art museums where this is possible, at least in some degree. I would go further myself, and advocate that it should be applied to re-unite the fine arts with the rest. I am not saying that there should be a wholesale pooling of the resources of all art museums and galleries of painting to achieve this, because that is not practicable and perhaps not even desirable, but there is room for much more co-operation between the museums and the galleries and it would promote that re-integration of art with the community to which so much lip-service is being paid. It is one of the special charms of the Wallace Collection at Hertford House that French paintings are shown in association with furniture, porcelain and other *objets d'art* of their period. Even the most uninformed visitor in the course of a short walk can sense the transition from the régime of Louis XIV to his successor's, and the paintings, furniture, ormolu and Sèvres complement one another to produce the effect. There are of course many background 'irrelevances' at the Wallace Collection—Dutch and Spanish paintings, European and oriental armours—but the visual impact of an impression of the French Court would be hard to match in France itself, and one wonders just how much this has ever been exploited as an aid to history teaching. That museum contrivance, the 'period room', on the other hand, is artificial. My own feeling is that it is rarely successful. The old-fashioned period room either had three walls and an open front roped off from the public, or the public had to peep into it through a door or window, and it all looked quite dead or as dead as a stage-setting without the lights and the actors. It is possible to build an effective period room, but it costs a great deal of money. Apart from the fact that it is now rarely possible to obtain the necessary furnishings, including details like lamps and fire-irons, the walls and ceiling unless they can be removed from some convenient old house have to be reproduced in their entirety. Certain American museums such as the Metropolitan have been able to do this, and on a more modest scale Scandinavian museums have done it. Yet even money and the means to make full use of it will not put life into the result. The room never looks lived in unless one can create conditions such as there are at Winterthur which, although a museum and very highly organized as such, was and still is a country house. Here in season the windows may be thrown open, so that the sounds of birds and scent of blossom drift in, and the vases are filled with fresh-gathered flowers; but more important, there are no barriers, no shuffling public to dispel the illusion, since every visitor is individually conducted round like a house-guest.

What, in the ordinary city museum, is the alternative to the period room? It lies, I think, in the avoidance of any attempts to create illusion, in frank recognition that circumstances are arti-ficial. Then instead of painstaking attempts to assemble an in-terior scene doomed never to come alive, one is free to use one's existing resources to create on a larger scale groups symbolic of a period or style just as is done on a small scale inside the cases. The operative word is 'create'. Again we have to seek the taste and skill of the display artist, so to group the material that it evokes the spirit of a period, and there must be close under-standing and sympathy between him and the curatorial staff who have to supply him with information. And there is no doubt that to omit paintings from such group compositions would, in some cases, almost be to present Hamlet without the Prince of Denmark. A Dutch domestic grouping of the later seventeenth century, for example, would be wholly misleading without, shall we say, a De Hooch to open a window on the courtyard outside or a Kalf to introduce the harvest of the good earth to match the craftsman's achievement. But it is not necessarily the painting which brings life to a group formed from the decorative arts.

The decorative arts may do as much for a painting. An obvious example would be a Dutch still-life, grouped with pieces similar to some of those depicted—a flagon, it might be, or drinking glasses. Even a genre or a battle scene could be lent added interest by a well-mounted item of costume or a piece of armour. In rare cases it may be possible to show the actual object or objects in a painting: a silver tea-service perhaps, or a cup like the one by Adam van Vianen of Utrecht which I once had charge of, 'portraits' of which were in both a Dutch and an American museum.

Such links apart, even the greatest of paintings may benefit by association with one or two masterpieces of contemporary decorative art. There is an understandable tendency utterly to isolate outstanding paintings—the so-called 'Night Watch' in the Rijksmuseum, for example—and there is no doubt that they gain by separation from lesser paintings; but such isolation is of course contrived and a little unnatural, and might be achieved more sympathetically by companioning the painting with one or two related lovely things—Ghirlandaio's flaxen-haired girl in the National Gallery, say, with a Florentine marriage coffer, or some such evocative piece. Here and there it is done, but why not far more often? The more one thinks of it, the more ridiculous it seems almost everywhere to perpetuate this divorce of things which once belonged together just because doing something about it would annoy a few sticklers for tradition. All works of art belong with a background, are full of allusions to it. When Kenneth Clark wrote that he could not enjoy a pure aesthetic experience for longer than he could enjoy the smell of an orange he was referring to the importance of historical criticism as an enhancement to a painting, and I believe an attempt to indicate appropriate environment or context by means of other art objects has similar value, particularly for the less scholarly museum visitor.

This problem of re-marrying the arts and their display in appropriate environments brings us to a movement which has gathered momentum in recent years: the historic house, perhaps more commonly now called the 'stately home'. Should this not have a place in any re-thinking about museums? There has been so much talk of such places as going commerical concerns, particularly when associated with ancillary attractions as at Longleat or Woburn, that one tends to forget they contain a very high proportion of the nation's artistic heritage. And their treasures comprise both the decorative and the fine arts in the sort of balance and environment which I have been advocating.

At the risk of going over more old ground, it should be emphasized here that popular indifference to the arts in this country is fostered not only by the 'class' distinctions which we have allowed to divide the arts, but also and more evidently by the popular impression that art in general is something which is the concern not of Us, but of Them. Spontaneous movements seeking to generate natural forms of artistic expression have been growing, especially among young people, with returns to folk music and cults like 'Pop', and the need to separate art from privilege is widely recognized, by the Arts Councils among others, though this sometimes leads them into strange errors merely substituting the privilege of the 'expert' for the privileges of birth, money and education. Undoubtedly the new movements have stimulated the interest of young people in our art museums, as they have stimulated their interest in concert-going, in the theatre and in the philosophical and sociological topics covered by a vast paperback output.

But popular though they may think themselves, those new movements and attitudes do not begin to touch the solid core of the people. And when I insist that museums have grown in popularity, it is obvious there are tens of millions of people in this country who never pass through the doors of an art museum or gallery and would never dream of doing so. Yet many of them find their ways to the stately homes. It may be claimed they go go for the wrong reasons: idle curiosity, a place to make for in the car at week-ends, the fun and games in an unusual setting which some great houses offer, the chance to bump into a duke. But most of them do file through the salons and up the staircase and even listen to what the guides have to tell them if those guides are persuasive, and some of this pageantry of past cultures does rub off on them though their memories may be muddled. There are museum men and women who think that this has nothing to do with what museums are trying to do, certainly nothing to do with education however elementary.

Where does education begin? It would be a mistake to underrate the possibilities of those historic houses, however little the average visitor may seem to learn by visiting them. They may offer a break-through where the art apathy-barrier is concerned. There is often quite a holiday atmosphere, and people who come are not subdued by an aura of learning. Probably they are bewildered by so much aristocratic art, but at least it is instantly meaningful for them, the outward expression of a way of life, however remote from their own. It is not art in the abstract, and that is a beginning. They may envy its owners, or feel them to be alien and therefore hostile, the reaction aimed at in some post-revolutionary museums in the U.S.S.R. when they labelled displays 'Art of the nineteenth-century Bourgeoisie' or some such thing. But that art was important to the people who built and lived in those houses and fostered a great number of craftsmen they could not doubt.

The historic house 'movement' has spread since the war, in the earlier stages on the initiative of owners, as an expedient to delay the destruction of great properties by the social revolution. Such destruction has been far more serious than most people realize, amounting to perhaps three of four hundred houses in the last quarter of a century. The position was made very clear by an exhibition at the Victoria and Albert Museum in 1974. The attitude to this situation expressed in the Green Paper on the Wealth Tax in the same year was one of anxiety about the national heritage which, it is hoped, will become 'more readily available to the public generally'. Certainly those houses are a national asset of great value. We have taken a long time to recognize what was obvious, and the pressing need now is to save this heritage and then to see it is appreciated. It is going to cost money, and much thought and effort. I do not think we should over-organize or have everything administered by some distant authority in a rigid fashion; but at the moment there is a state of confusion, ranging from blinkered indifference to a frenzied scramble for contributions from a variety of financial sources, with owners unaware from year to year of what the future may hold. The exceptional owner is an astute businessman and has made the property he has inherited earn at least a substantial proportion of its running costs, but he has to be vigilant or one morning he and we will wake up to find that a heritage which is both his and ours is again under threat. We are so apt to forget those houses are part of *our* birthright too. And it might be asked whether such an owner should have to introduce exotic irrelevances like safari parks and fun-fairs to render his house and its contents a viable enterprize. Is it not rather like introducing a bingo hall into the National Gallery?

If those houses are precious to us, they are precious as they stand and where possible they should be underwritten by sums sufficient to maintain them alive and free and not as part of a kind of menagerie. The Department of the Environment meticulously looks after the setting of its ancient monuments and rightly allocates considerable expenditure to their lawns and gardens when they possess such features. It is even more important to preserve our habitable monuments, and to preserve them as going concerns, sometimes even to having horses in the stables and peaches in the conservatory. The Americans, no doubt because they have fewer of those places and therefore value them more, neglect no detail. It is not the least of the attractions at Mount Vernon, Washington's old home in Virginia, that even herbs in the kitchen garden seem to be tended carefully, so that one feels the President might be back at any moment.

Here, of course, we are not concerned primarily with the problem of safeguarding our country houses in general. That has been surveyed admirably by the Cornforth Report. What we have to deal with, briefly, is how such houses relate to the future of museums, and there seem to be two main areas where the interests of museums and the great houses overlap.

The first area of interest is the contents of the houses. Whether a house is abandoned or not, its treasures are in danger. When Hamilton Palace was demolished last century an entire major gallery of the fine and decorative arts was dispersed across the world, but many surviving mansions—Belsay, Ashburnham Place, Croome Court and a score or two of others among the greater places alone—have lost the whole or part of their possessions. Such losses dismay our museums only less than—and occasionally more than!—the owners. Museums can only now and then hope to save by acquiring it something which a great house loses. Most museums regard the furnished mansions of this country as a sort of extension of their own collections and activities, always there for reference as well as enjoyment. Their card-indexes and catalogues record particulars of relevant material, and so do their photographic departments strive to have prints or negatives of things in private hands.

147

The second area of interest is just how far those houses are viable as actual museums. Here again the limits of our concern must be repeated: not the rescue of all those thousands of threatened houses but, sadly, only how their museum potentialities might save a certain number, if perhaps a larger number than at first might be imagined. A few already have been taken over by the State and are administered by national museums: Apsley House in London, for example, and Osterley Park and Ham House, these last leased from the National Trust. Local authorities have taken over places such as Temple Newsam House close to Leeds, and Heaton Hall and Platt Hall in the Manchester area, the latter now a noted costume museum. Several have come into the hands of the National Trust and the National Trust for Scotland, either directly or through the agency of the Government, which has accepted buildings and contents in lieu of death duties. Those houses are virtually museums, on their own or as parts of a municipal complex of museums. While State or local authority ownership does usually ensure efficient curating, inevitably there is a tendency to make the house fit into the conventional museum pattern. This no doubt was the target of V. Sackville-West's reference in *The English Country House*: 'Museums? A museum is a dead thing; a house which is still a home of men and women is a living thing which has not lost its soul.' And the same criticism came from Mr Arthur Woodburn at a conference on the country house which I attended in Edinburgh: 'We want to preserve living history, not dead museums.'

While noting the usual unfamiliarity with what the modern museum is about, one must admit those views are, in context, right. If the museum pattern means barriers and direction-signs and uniformed warders it will not do. The house becomes institutionalized. National Trust properties tend to come nearer the Sackville-West requirement, in part perhaps because local initiatives and enthusiasm have the chance to express themselves. In some cases the Trusts arrive at an arrangement with former owners whereby they and their families continue to live in the houses, possibly occupying only a few rooms. No doubt some extremists look on such an arrangement as a perpetuation of privilege which should be ended ruthlessly; but, as I heard it put rather neatly at the conference mentioned, one must distinguish between maintenance of our heritage and maintenance of the status quo, and if a modest element of family continuity can help to foster the spirit of this stimulating fight to preserve what is best in our past then prejudice should get short shrift. The Trusts may not always welcome the arrangement. Families must frequently resent the takeover, resent interference by Trust officers who may wish to suppress features which they consider inappropriate or to introduce others to emphasize the character of the house; but ideally a resident family seems the right way to keep an old house 'alive'.

I believe, then, that we should seriously consider the possibility, over a longish period, of recruiting many of our town and country mansions as extensions of the museum system, with the primary function of displaying furnishings, the decorative arts and the appropriate paintings and sculpture in the settings for which they were made or where at least they belong. As to paintings, portraits in particular come to mind. Not only do all those things retain a dimension and meaning which they must lose when extracted and presented, however beautifully, in a great museum, but this could be an answer to the complaint that such treasures are concentrated in our cities, London above all. If I seem to be dreaming of a network of mansions from Land's End to John o' Groats competing with one another for the custom of a peripatetic public and eventually growing stale and losing their impact, I can only say there is small danger of public interest waning. In this small country present trends are such that people look eagerly for such oases, and the 'developers' seem all too likely to intensify those trends. In some areas the danger could be an over-popularity which would threaten the essential atmosphere.

Earlier in this book it is suggested that museums, for some, are almost a kind of spiritual sanctuary. The country house museum would offer a similar kind of sanctuary, and probably to far more, even mute sermons on values to the growing number who are dismayed by the values imposed by the affluent society. I am not thinking of stately homes alone, but of pleasant country vicarages and the modest homes of squires and lairds who, in spite of limited incomes, over the generations contrived to surround themselves with goods and chattels and small works of art which would now fetch high prices at Christie's or Sotheby's. Here art is without a capital 'A' and, disarmed by the scent of

149

mown lawns and stocks drifting in through the casements, people will accept it for what it is. It is a daunting task to try to preserve any people's heritage through a social revolution—France lost a major part of hers and has to look for it now in the museums of other lands—yet financially it would probably be more than covered by the wage-increases of one inflationary year. It may be that the museums should exercise some type of stewardship over all those scattered houses, vulnerable both to crime and carelessness; and if responsibility is to be divided along present lines, here with outright private ownership continuing as long as it can, there with the National Trusts taking over, there again with central or local government stepping in, some sort of co-ordinating body will be required. But this is both a problem and an opportunity unique to Britain. As the Cornforth Report remarks, country houses with all their landed appurtenances reflect a centuries-old aspect of the British way of life. It is by identifying itself with such imaginative projects that the museum movement can help to prove its new attitudes to the community.

XVI The Local Museum

THE WORDS 'local museum' have an almost apologetic ring about them. They conjure up memories of neglected little buildings, of ventures born perhaps of the nineteenth-century passion for improvement, the initial momentum and the contents of which have been deteriorating ever since. It is hardly surprising that in a time of new thinking about museums, some people should be in favour of 'rationalizing' the local museum out of existence because it only serves to give the museum movement a bad name. I would go so far as to agree that there are too many local museums, and that some of them are trying to do the wrong things and that too many more have no policy at all; but in principle the local museum has a vital part to play in the modernization of the museum service.

The adjective 'local' is the first stumbling block. In a paper read to a conference in New York State many years ago Dr Parr surveys the alternatives and settles for 'indigenous', although almost at once he expresses dissatisfaction with that too. The truth is that the local museum can be so many sorts of thing, depending upon where it finds itself and whom it serves, that no word is quite appropriate over all. The one thing it is not is a major museum writ small. I would define it as a small town or country museum concerned primarily with local affairs.

Not so many years ago it became widely accepted that a local museum should concern itself with local things almost to the exclusion of the wider world. Museum authorities were troubled by the fact that so many small museums had grown up around heterogeneous collections given or bequeathed to them by local collectors, collections which had no particular relevance to the district and which more often than not had been amassed without any plan and too often with little real knowledge of what was being collected. We all know this kind of museum. I recall one in particular whose contents ranged from late Imari porcelain and iron cannon balls to an alligator hanging stiffly from rusty chains in a gallery rendered dangerous by dry-rot, memorials of a much-travelled local doctor, and for all its fascination there could be no quarrel with the decision to dismantle it. It was a monument to the idiosyncracies of one man of magpie propensities, long dead: such meaning as it may have had when he was there to talk about it had faded like the plumage of the parrots in one of its dusty cases.

Yet the district in which this curious building lay is rich in history and prehistory, and not fifteen miles away is another little museum which, because of the enterprise and scholarship of its curator, has become a treasure house of local lore, fully documented and duly described, in many instances, in the appropriate journals. This second place certainly fits the prescription for a local museum as laid down between the wars: rich in information both for residents and for visitors. Its weakness is that in spite of systematic arrangement and the contribution it has made to knowledge of the district, its success again relies too much on the enthusiasm of one man, informed though he is, so that when he goes his invaluable material may well gather dust as happened in the neighbouring museum. The lesson is that the local museum must achieve the state of being an organic part of the community, functioning with and adapting to its life.

For the curators of many small museums the luxury of a policy is a dream beyond realization. It takes them all their time to keep the place wind and water tight. Sir John Myres in a British Association publication of 1944 pleads for the curator to be freed from 'mere custody and maintenance' so that he can pursue 'a positive and active policy and programme of public service'. But even to discover the needs of so many and such scattered museums was itself a formidable task undertaken over many years under the auspices of the Museums Association and the Carnegie United Kingdom Trust. The result of the surveys, reports and money spent was the cleaning up of many of those local museums, some modernization in a physical sense, sometimes an improvement in the staffing position. The larger museums helped where they could, notably with the conservation and identification of specimens. But there can have been few instances in which the changes wrought were extended to a lasting new relationship with the community. It was possible as lately as 1970 for a letter to appear in the *Museums Journal* from the senior assistant in a London museum of local history begging the Association itself to wake up to the local museum's needs. Much as may have been thought and written about our local museums, no exciting new thinking has emerged to compare with the new thinking in the larger institutions. Even Coleman in America in his *Manual for Small Museums* makes no attempt to evolve a philosophy.

The basic problem with the local museum is that everyone in the community who is interested must know all he wants to know about the entire contents after a visit or two, so that no matter how well presented those contents may be, there will be few visitors in the course of a year, outsiders apart. In an area of high tourist attraction this may not appear to be so serious, as in summer at least the museum will be serving a useful purpose. But tourists should be no more than a credit bonus. The primary job which a public museum has to do, no matter what its size, is for the community it serves. What can the small museum do to keep up the interest, to keep people coming back as they do to the public library? I have said more than once that things must always be happening in a museum, and be seen to be happening, but in a small museum this looks to be an impossibility.

Dr Parr in the paper already referred to asserts it is one of the museum's most important functions to teach people to see. One unhappy result of modern improvements in communications is that more and more people look further and further off for things to interest them. They are growing more restless and more discontented with their own environment than ever before. Standardization of goods and chattels, of homes, pressures by mass media and advertising directing choices of nearly everything that is marketed: all those things tend to a blunting of apprehension, a deprivation of experience, which are behind many of our social problems. Too many of us are thinking in clichés and content to accept other people's views and decisions. As Dr Parr points out, it is not our eyes that see: they only make sight possible. We have to get back to a condition of *awareness*, rediscover the pleasures of learning, probe for ourselves the secrets of our own environment, if as a people we are to achieve the pursuit of happiness in the profound sense of the words of the Declaration of Independence. Dr Parr believes that what he calls the indigenous museum can do much to promote this. It can do it better than any large museum with wide responsibilities can.

I have warned about the danger of the one-man museum declining when that man and his enthusiasm go, but leadership in a small museum is bound to be a very personal affair, and the hope must be that he establish a pattern for his successors, and a demand for it in the community. It is through his eyes that the environment will be scrutinized and through his mind that it will be interpreted. Unless he can experience and pass on the thrill of discovery his museum will remain unvisited, and deservedly so. To find the right men for all the local museums that exist sounds like a counsel of perfection, but there is no doubt that without creative curatorship of this kind there is small chance of the local museum justifying itself. Stock, off-the-peg advice will not save it. It is not enough to concentrate on pottery in the Potteries, on fishing in a fishing-port, and to instal row upon row of bowls and tea-services or of model fishing-smacks, no matter how carefully chosen and labelled and displayed. Human problems and satisfactions in plenty lie behind those end-products, and they must get through to the visitor and kindle his interest and curiosity. Once interest is fully aroused it can be enticed in all sorts of directions: from simple pots to the chemistry of glazes or theories of aesthetics, from fisheries now to the future harvest of the sea. If simply devised, those follow-up displays may be changed several times a year, perhaps to fit events—the impact of oil on the fishing-grounds, for example.

Such changes make great demands on the curator. And visual displays alone are not enough to keep a small museum alive: there must be talks by people with something to say, film-shows not merely of stock reels from a library, but as often as possible closely relevant to the district's interests, discussion groups, meetings of societies connected with the museum's field or fields. Most of those things cost money, but of that I will say something presently. If the museum has not a local industry to reflect, and perhaps to support it, there is still the duty to make the local visitor look hard at his environment. Dr Parr draws attention to the heightened enjoyment of a walk through the woods by someone for whom the hundreds of things seen are meaningful. All that many curators do about this is to show a case or two of local butterflies or birds' eggs, with or without comment on where to look for them. The very least he must do is to relate the butterflies to food-plants and relate those to each changing season as it comes round, spotlighting what can be seen and where at any particular time, examining the life-cycle, commenting, say, on the effects of fen-drainage or of agricultural innovations. In the case of birds he may consider tape-recording bird-calls month by month. If the district is one rich in prehistory he may find it less easy to introduce an element of change, unless there are current excavations of importance, but if he is engrossed in his subject there are always new things to say, even if he uses local pegs on which to hang related news from another district, another country.

The importance of the temporary exhibition in the large museum has been discussed (in Chapter XIV). In the smaller local museum it is a rarity, yet it is even more important here. The pressing need to maintain the interest of a small community demands a succession of events, and if the premises are adequate there must be an attempt to insure that it is in the museum such events, where appropriate, are to be looked for rather than in, say, the village hall which probably does not need such things as exhibitions to supplement the meetings and dances, badminton and concerts, which justify it anyway. The Arts Council, the Council of Industrial Design, the Rural Industries Council and many other organizations mount travelling exhibitions which they are only too ready to 'place' where they can find a suitable home for them. The Museums Regional Federations also have their travelling exhibitions, and so have the circulation departments of the Victoria and Albert and the Science Museums. Here I would slip in a *caveat*: while many of those centrally organized exhibitions are good, they are not normally made to measure, and some of them inevitably have an 'off-the-peg' look which is more obvious in a small museum where such exhibitions are so much more prominent. Their relevance too has to be considered. Not that a small-town or rural community should be expected to have no interest in a selection of Bohemian glass or West African wood-carvings, but to lean too heavily upon stock circulating exhibitions brings the local museum back to the point where we came in—the museum of irrelevant curiosities. There is also the question of space. Few local museums can afford to devote a portion of their premises permanently to a succession of changing events. But where possible at all it is worth a sacrifice to have one large room available. It could double its function and serve as lecture theatre and cinema, perhaps also as the meeting-place of the antiquarian or natural history society. To keep things happening is more important than having all the permanent collections on show all the time.

There has been passing reference to talks or lectures as a means of sustaining interest. It has astonished me at times how little enterprize and energy are devoted to making these a success where such things are held at all. It should be less difficult to arrange lectures and discussions in a small community than in a large one where there is stiff competition from other events, but as often as not the visiting lecturer is greeted with an apology because his lecture clashes with a Women's Rural Association meeting or the A.G.M. of the golf-club. Perhaps the biggest problem will be to generate the momentum to carry a series of lectures through from year to year as something to which people look forward. No one will expect to see big names on the syllabus. Big names do not necessarily spell success. An ability to talk interestingly about subjects not too remote from the audience's experience is far more likely to bring people back to hear the next talk than would a celebrity with an indifferent capacity to communicate. It would be of immense service to curators, and indeed to the secretaries of local societies, if panels of suitable men and women available in a region could be compiled by some competent body, perhaps the local authority or a university. Even if no fee were possible—and it rarely is!—I believe there are enough people ready and able to talk on their own subject to fill the syllabus each year; but they will not do it if they meet with the sort of slipshod organization too often experienced. This is much more discouraging than the absence of a fee.

While the curator of a local museum must give the main part of his time and energy to holding the attention of the community and rousing their interest, this does not mean he need neglect research. The curator of the little museum referred to early in this chapter deservedly received an honorary degree from a distant university, and there are many others like him devoted to study of their area. It has been claimed for local museums that they feed the larger institutions with specialized information which they need to build up a total picture: in fact that they are the eyes and ears of the great central museums. To some extent this is true. It would be even more true if local museums were freed from what at present is too often a hand-to-mouth existence, and by help with staffing, money and equipment were enabled to fulfil all their possible functions instead of having to choose between them.

If any reader connected with a local museum has persevered up to this point, it will be with mounting impatience at exhortations to do things which under existing circumstances just cannot be done. Devotion can achieve much, but in the long run there is no substitute for money. Many local museums have not the backing of a local authority: they may be dependent on a society or trust whose funds and membership have dwindled. Even where a local authority is responsible, it may be ignorant of what can be done with a museum and look on it as a liability, leaving matters to a librarian who is probably *ex officio* curator and without enthusiasm for his unwanted charge. The situation has improved, but few authorities have the vision to see what a substantial increase in funds could achieve. To most of them, a museum is just a museum. The ratepayers are unlikely to put pressure on them as they might over lack of library facilities. There has to be pressure, and help, from outside. The Bow Group publication has as its first principal recommendation a National Museum System, 'administered by a National Museums Authority with powers to co-ordinate the activities of museums, both regional and national'. Earlier this is interpreted as involving a national regional museum in every region, with powers to co-ordinate all museums within its territory. This plan is intended to be the vehicle of what the author, Donald Adamson, calls 'the museums rescue operation'.

The need for a 'rescue operation' is certainly urgent for local museums, and the idea of a nation-wide service involving co-operation at all levels has been discussed for years within the profession itself. The Museums Association has published a number of proposals submitted by its Council to the 1971 annual conference. In summary, their proposals are not unlike those of the Bow Group publication of a month or two earlier, involving a 'vertical' system whereby assistance and funding are supplied through the national museums in the top tier to 'provincial national' and regional museums, which in turn would support smaller museums in their areas. Local museums are not dealt with in this paper, except to say they could call upon assistance, although remaining autonomous, 'unless they wished to enter

F

into a formal agreement with the regional museum or museums'. To help the small museums first, it is maintained, would be to begin at the wrong end. The contention is that it is the larger institutions which need to be strengthened, so that they can help with the lesser ones in their area.

The theory of a national museums service on these lines on the face of it looks reasonable, yet one is left speculating how far it would meet the needs of the case. To begin at what the report calls the wrong end, there are some local museums the collections, and indeed the very fabric, of which may have disintegrated by the time an efficient national and regional service has been built up to the point where they might ask for its help, far less receive it. I am uneasy, too, about results being dependent on the deliberations of committees, perhaps tiers of committees, some of whose members could be more argumentative than knowledgeable. Not only are conditions of local museums deteriorating all the time; new communities are growing like mushrooms from urban overspill, outlooks are changing, loyalties between new and old elements in communities are under strain, chances offered that must be grasped at once or lost. We all know of small towns which have had 'new towns' thrust upon them. Whether they are dormitory satellites of cities or have their own industrial 'infrastructure'—to fall back upon planners' jargon—they produce critical and often discontented populations without community sense, and a decaying museum in their midst would be finished off by the gangs. On the other hand, a progressive museum could be one of the focus-points of the effort to create identity and contentment. No: there are many local museums which cannot wait.

What local museums need is the right men, some advice, and some money, and they need those now. In certain cases they have the right man; all he needs is the money. Yet money, in a sense, is the least difficult need. The Bow Group's second recommendation was a central Government grant of £10 million over a limited period for rebuilding regional museums. Nothing was said about local museums, but a sum which would hardly be noticed in terms of normal public expenditure could solve at least the physical problems of the neediest of our local museums, and enable their curators to do some positive planning. There would have to be assurances that the money would be used efficiently, with a lively awareness of the needs of the situation.

158

How it should be allocated is the first problem. The Regional Federations have a fairly complete picture and could investigate appeals, or the larger museums in an area might do so, much as the Victoria and Albert and Royal Scottish Museums do now in administering the grants-in-aid for purchases by non-national museums. The important thing is not to wait until a new administrative body is devised and set up.

As to advice, advice on how to apply the money, on whether a local museum has the right man in charge of it, in the present urgent situation there could be a case for one or two small roving commissions to proceed to the places of greatest need, composed of only two or three people combining the necessary experience with vision to see the possibilities of a situation. They would report back to whatever body administered the available funds. There might in fact be a place for such commissions in the long term as well as the short. Looking further ahead, I believe there is a strong case for putting the present loose relationship between the big central museums and the smaller on a firmer basis, even for temporary exchanges of staff; but at the same time I believe that too rigid a hierarchy in a total national museum service could result in local museums, in exchange for increased efficiency, losing their character and the vitality which ideally all should possess.

XVII The Folk Museum

IN BRITAIN the folk museum is still something rather new. A very small proportion of the population has ever entered one, or perhaps even heard of such a thing. To some people the notion may be slightly comical, something that belongs to the world of maypoles and Morris dancers or that peasant way of life which seems quite foreign to us. But in fact we should do well to look more closely at the folk museum movement. The philosophy behind it contains certain lessons for us—particularly for us, because when we bent ourselves to the Industrial Revolution we dislocated our national backbone and, culturally and indeed in other ways, have been suffering for it ever since.

Folk museums are essentially a northern idea. They were the passion of Artur Hazelius of Stockholm, but their roots go much further back in time, probably to Olof Rudbeck of Uppsala who, born two years after the death of Gustavus Adolphus and with his imagination borne high on the wave of that king's conquests, insisted that the genius of Europe stemmed from northern soil. Gustavus himself revered his country's past: the present office of the Royal Custodian of Antiquities in Sweden was created by him. In the nineteenth century in Sweden the Romantic Revival released a deep interest in tradition, especially in dialects and folk-songs, and in 1873 this led to Hazelius founding Nordiska Museet, which expressed the pan-Scandinavian sentiment sweeping his country. Nordiska Museet was, and still is, the great centre for Nordic folk art. Less than twenty years later came the first true folk museum. It was laid out upon a hill in Stockholm called Skansen, and took this for its name, becoming the model for most of the other museums of its kind.

Scandinavia was exceptionally well equipped to carry out the folk museum idea. It had not suffered urbanization, and not only the country districts but also the towns had great numbers of old buildings still in use. It is a heavily timbered region, and wood

160

was the principle building material. Wood encourages not only a wide variety of stylistic treatment, marking out one province clearly from another, but also spontaneous embellishment by the wood-carver, so that a rural wooden building generally has more obvious appeal to the eye than a corresponding building of stone or brick, to decorate which requires deliberation and time and costs money. Then it is a much simpler matter to dismantle a wooden building and to transport and re-erect it on a museum site. Possibly another advantage which Scandinavia possesses is the long northern winter; because whereas in many other European countries winter is a rather dreary off-season where outdoor entertainments are concerned, the Swedes and Norwegians have made the most of deep snow and long, dark nights. Winter customs and festivals are therefore as popular as summer ones at Skansen. A folk museum which has to close down for six or seven months of the year is handicapped from the start.

The Skansen plan involved not merely bringing together groups of picturesque houses in a rural setting, but assembling as many types of house and of building techniques as were necessary to give an overall picture of the country's peasant living conditions. And to house and farm were added church, inns, market stalls, then a section of a town. But the success of Skansen —and its visitors total something around three millions per year in a city a quarter of this size—derives from a policy of infusing the place with life and stir. It houses craftsmen who actually ply their old trades: potters, glass-workers, tanners, bakers, printers, a goldsmith. Old country festivals are celebrated. There is a zoo for indigenous and other animals. More recently the management has gone further and added a wide range of entertainments from skating and skiing to children's playgrounds and industrial exhibitions. To my way of thinking, they have gone too far. Skansen has lost a little of a certain quality which can be found in other Scandinavian folk museums of more recent foundation; but they may well argue that over-popularization is far better than neglect. And it is to be remembered that Skansen is very much a serious museum, a partner with Nordiska Museet, with massive archives and library and a formidable reputation for scholarship.

The term 'folk museum' itself offers a wide choice of interpretations and approaches, but unless 'folk' has ceased to have any meaning, popularity is an essential aim. What, then, is the real significance of such a museum? Conservation and research apart, we know the purpose of an ordinary museum is education. Just how important is the sort of education which a folk museum can provide: important, I mean, for the ordinary man, woman and child? Even in Scandinavia, so far as the public is concerned, some folk museums appear to be no more than pleasant parks diversified by quaint dwellings. One of my favourites is Frilandsmuseet at Lyngby, on the outskirts of Copenhagen. There is a pretty windmill on a knoll and a watermill in a wooded dell, and there are colourful cottages from all over Denmark and farmsteads with beams bent and twisted with age, and when you are weary of walking there is a pleasant restaurant by the roadside. But this is hardly popular entertainment, and the annual total of visitors is less than a twentieth of Skansen's. Then in Norway there is the Norsk Folkemuseum at Bygdøy, a suburb of the capital at the head of the Oslofjord. It is entered through an impressive copy of the old town gate. Beyond is a group of buildings with conventional museum galleries, and beyond this again a park of thirty-five acres with regional groups of rural buildings and also a town group—a fine recreational facility for the citizens of Oslo enhanced by the close proximity of the Viking Ship Museum, the Fram Museum containing Nansen's ship, and the Kon-Tiki Museum, all close to the fjord with its myriads of white sails in season. There is almost no end to those pleasant resorts: Den Gamle By at Aarhus, Kulturen at Lund, the Sandvig Collection at Lillehammer . . . But for the average visitor, are those anything more than unusually attractive public parks? Do they contribute to the community more than diversion and fresh air? Do they, in fact, as museums have a valid and vital function, or are they just the playthings of antiquarians and folklorists?

It must be said at once that in Scandinavia folk museums do have an important function, and for the people. Scandinavians, in spite of their appetite for travel and pioneering in far places, have roots deep in their own soil, and their past history does not seem to be a subject in which they have to force an interest. Festivals, whether of the solstices or the Christian calendar, still waken deep feelings in them. Patriotism in the old sense has not yet become a dirty word with them and they fly their national flags by the thousand on little excuse or none. They possess in their folk museums innumerable bygones because they have treasured them, where others would long ago have discarded them. They will make sacrifices for them because they are proud of them: how many other peoples of a few million souls would have faced up to the task and cost of raising and restoring the sunken *Vasa* as the Swedes have done? Folk museums come naturally to them.

For a different reason they seem to come naturally also to the people of the United States. Because they have a relatively short history and at the same time a need to assure themselves they have a real identity, they too treasure all their bygones—and this in a country which has taught the world the pernicious creed of 'built-in obsolescence'! The amount of surviving American 'colonial' furniture of a quality comparable with good English eighteenth-century pieces has to be seen to be believed. Apart from some early material like 'Pennsylvania Dutch', most of what comes into the folk-museum category in the United States, in Europe of course would not come into the folk category at all, and there was certainly no peasant class there at any time.

But we must accept that the definition of a folk museum does not limit it to peasant material alone, that 'folk' is the people in the ancient sense in which it has survived, for example, in the Folkething, the lower house of the Danish parliament. In this sense—and it is certainly the sense in which it is used in that pioneering institution Nordiska Museet—the material remains of any social class which has contributed to the people's identity is folk material. Farmsteads and workshops and burghers' houses may be most typical of the formative years of the north European nations; but in America the log-cabin or a pueblo dwelling are not really more significant than the fine home of a Virginia tobacco-planter or Jefferson's Monticello. Folk history in America is as complex as it is important to the build-up of the national personality. In Scandinavia there is only the complexity of regional variations, perhaps with one racial intrusion, the Lapps. In the United States the folk has been wrought from perhaps a score of European folk traditions: English, Scottish, Irish, Welsh, French, Spanish, German, Scandinavian, Italian and so on. In addition there are the native cultures. And there are great formative folk movements such as the drive west, no more to be omitted than New England Puritanism. It is small wonder that the importance of preserving those cultures and traditions has been accepted and underwritten by great sums of money, and that popular response has been widespread. Looked at from those two far different national angles, the folk museum's educational potential is not hard to see.

The need somehow to infuse old habitations and bygones with life, to make them articulate, is well recognized in the United States. At Cooperstown, New York State, the old trades are still plied by blacksmith, druggist, dairyman, and there are seminars on housewifery as well as instruction in the traditional crafts. At Mystic Seaport in Connecticut there is a complete seafaring village of New England, with old ships lying in harbour, and it is at once a centre of maritime history studies and a popular place of pilgrimage, rather like Bygdøy, with yacht club and an Age of Sail museum. But of course the most famous example of this type of museum in the United States is Colonial Williamsburg in Virginia now about half-a-century old. It is too well known to need description. The point to be stressed here is the determination from the start to make the town live, and to live at its own pace, that of a seventeenth-century community. Time, scholarship and money were lavished upon examination of every document available, as well as of every nail and potsherd dug up on the site, to establish precisely the pattern of life in colonial times, and not only was the town rebuilt on this firm foundation, but the people who were to live there virtually had to turn back the clock. Thus the blacksmith lives his daily life at the pace of the horses he shoes, the druggist discusses the simples he uses and their virtues as if modern drugstores did not exist, and the silversmith takes no latter-day short-cuts in raising and decorating the tankards and other domestic wares which he makes and sells. It would be ridiculous to suggest that the citizens of rebuilt Williamsburg have shut the modern world out completely, but their outlook is certainly conditioned by the old standards, whether the things they live with are the work of one of their contemporaries and neighbours like the silversmith, or of their forerunners, either nameless or legendary like Paul Revere or the Englishman Thomas Tompion who made the ninety-day clock in the Governor's Palace gleaming white under the old-style Union Jack at the masthead. There are purists who criticize Williamsburg because it is mainly replica; but what we have to ask is what the experience of coming here does for the half-million or so visitors who arrive every year. For most of them I suspect it is unforgettable, like the first day or two in a foreign country.

Motives which encouraged the folk museum movement in the United States and Scandinavia were not present, at least in the same degree, in Britain. Destruction of great areas of rural life, replacement of an agricultural by an urban economy, looking to other lands for its raw materials, made what remained of 'England's green and pleasant land' more of a playground or a nostalgic dream for the majority, and until quite recent years the collecting of bygones was a mere sentimental pastime, certainly not a matter for academic preoccupation. As to the larger museums, their huge ethnographical collections were mainly concerned with the bygones of 'primitive' peoples. Sir Henry Miers in his *Report on the Public Museums of the British Isles* (1928) remarks that by contrast with the period houses illustrating the life of the wealthier classes there is nothing to illustrate the life of the workers.

Things were, however, beginning to move. Only eight years later an economic historian of growing repute, Dr I. F. Grant, completed a collecting survey of the Scottish Highlands and Islands and opened Britain's first folk museum on Iona. She gave it the name of Am Fasgadh, The Shelter, and a few years later transferred it by way of Laggan to Kingussie in Inverness-shire. It was very small, with only two or three cottages. In 1955 a grant from the Pilgrim Trust enabled it to be taken over by the (now) four older Scottish universities.

Two years after Am Fasgadh came to Kingussie, the most ambitious of Britain's folk museums began with the gift by the Earl of Plymouth of the castle and grounds of St Fagan's to the National Museum of Wales. This has grown as Am Fasgadh has been unable to do. Funds and staff have been made available to it, and the close proximity of Cardiff has insured a very fair flow of visitors. If a folk museum is to be a really viable proposition, it must be close to a large centre of population. Williamsburg is an exception, but it has grown into something like a national monument and is served by its own group of hotels without the precincts. St Fagan's, like Bygdøy, is a recreational facility for the neighbouring city. But again like the Scandinavian folk museums, it is an important study centre for scholars interested in folk art, dialects, music, dancing, and possesses archives and a large library.

In the wake of those two pioneering ventures in the 'Celtic Fringe', the folk museum movement is expanding. Blaise Castle serves the Bristol and southwestern area, with special emphasis on agriculture, and agriculture again is the main theme of the Museum of English Rural Life at Reading, under the auspices of the University. The West Yorkshire Museum at Halifax is a complex centred on a manor house fully furnished with seventeenth-century pieces. And although a folk museum only in the sense that it does illustrate aspects of 'the life of the workers', there is the highly successful open-air museum of industrial archaeology at Ironbridge Gorge, in Shropshire. Scotland has been slow to follow up Miss Grant's initiative, but there are a few small ventures such as the Angus Folk Museum at Glamis, confined to a row of cottages, and the National Museum of Antiquities is amassing what must be a considerable collection with a view to a national folk museum. Ulster has achieved its National Folk Museum at Holywood, just outside Belfast. Well founded academically though these British enterprises are, and attractive as they may be to visit, my feeling, however, is that communities here have not yet begun to be aware of their potential significance and still regard them as refuges for a cult of bygones.

I hope I do not seem to be casting a cold eye on a great deal of enterprize and enthusiasm if I say that the folk museum movement has passed beyond the stage of being a rescue operation and has to be subjected to some critical scrutiny in the light of its social function, as we have been doing with other museums for a generation and more. Perhaps even in Scandinavia the time may have come to take a new look at it, to ask whether the very real interest in traditional arts and customs may not begin to wane unless there are growth-points from which it can continue to develop. While the folk museum, in this country now as well as in others, fulfils the requirements of a modern museum in standards of conservation and research, in the field of education, particularly popular education, it poses a number of questions.

Putting myself in the shoes of the average lay visitor, I am bound to say that a succession of rural dwellings, farms, mills, workshops leaves a very blurred impression, and a succession of folk museums blurs memories even more. Sharp as the contrast may be at the time between a timber farmhouse from Dalarna

166

province and a half-timbered one from Skåne, it is not likely to remain long in the memory of an ordinary Stockholm citizen, far less of a British or American visitor to Skansen. Why should it? In any case, folk museums are not as informative as other museums are. There has to be minimum labelling if exhibits are meant to look natural and lived-in, and guidebooks and general group-labels only interrupt the slightly euphoric mood created by colourful houses embowered in spring blossom or autumn leaves. It is much easier to learn something, of course, from the mills and the craft-workshops where men and women are actually doing things: operating the cumbrous but amazingly efficient wooden machinery that grinds the corn, using the looms, shoeing the horses. Yet even this could be called just animated antiquarianism, peepshows on the past. What is there in it for the community of today?

Victorian enthusiasm for museums stemmed from the earnest belief that they could help teach things which would improve the quality of life, whether through an understanding of nature, or of technology or of beauty. The life represented by the folk museum is a relatively uncomplicated one, in mansion house as in cottage. Other museums tend to single out more sophisticated artifacts for display, particularly in art—as Miers so frankly emphasized. Much of what the folk museum shows is basic, and the skills which it illustrates in its workshops are the basic skills of epochs when men got most of their satisfactions from their own craft or from their appreciation of the craft of others whom every day they could see plying their trades. We have come a long way from Cobbett's *Cottage Economy*, and today those who follow up his philosophy are sometimes attacked as romantics; yet the 'great wen' outlook which he reviled as destroying England seems like to do so and has brought us to a point at which most of us are looking about us in uncertainty, if not dread.

Western civilization has hitched its waggon to a star called better living-standards, which it measures mainly in terms of domestic appliances and shorter hours of work. How *should* we measure them? As our art museums are custodians of what is best in art, why should our folk museums, our museums of the folk, not be the custodians of what is excellent in the basic things we surround ourselves with, and clothe ourselves in, and eat and drink and divert ourselves with? I think they might take on a watch-dog function for all the human skills which come within their province. Let them make—and sell—bread and cheeses as they should be made, let them cure hams and bacon by the old methods, let them cook and offer in their inns food to whet the jaded appetites of city visitors—without any of the alternative modern menus which some of them now timidly put on the tables. Let them likewise offer sanctuary to the numerous artist-craftsmen who are setting themselves up all over the country in response to the growing public dissatisfaction with the quality of monopoly goods and the big stores. Already some new-town planning authorities are trying to attract those people to them—how much more appropriate if their growing colonies were in the folk museums, where they have so much to give to the environment, and it to them. There they could be part of a conspiracy for the rediscovery of quality in living. There is no need for the silver-smiths to stick to the old shapes, for the glass-blowers to keep to the old styles, so long as they all match up to the old standards. Well, it may be a romantic notion, but it is a logical step along the path the folk museums are already following.

XVIII *Postscript: the Future of Museums*

IT HAS been suggested this book should be completed by an attempt to plot the course museums might take to the year 2000. Fifty years ago one might have imitated meteorologists by searching for patterns and cycles of change in the past and applying these to the next twenty-five years with some hope that the exercise might prove accurate in general terms. I would have grave doubts about the usefulness of this now. There is an ample literature to lengthen our vistas, as Dr Alma Wittlin puts it; but I feel that the very amplitude of the literature and the complex output of new ideas about museums make forecasting their future more rather than less uncertain. And we have to consider a social context in which anything could happen. Many museums have development plans, phased over a longish period, but will they be implemented in anything like their present shape—or, we may ask, should they be? Social and political pressures could make a nonsense of them and, if the inflationary factor persists, this could make a nonsense of how to fund them.

The ivory-tower existence of museums has been challenged, and rightly so, for a long time. Already the challenge has brought many responses and changes. But until quite recently it has been a challenge within a more or less stable society, and now that society itself is challenged with a new urgency on profound issues, moral issues such as that materialism towards which Marxism every bit as much as Capitalism has impelled us all. Prophets of hope, from Gandhi on to the present, in the interest of survival have envisaged such radical changes in social attitudes, industrial structures and scales of values that I find it difficult to imagine how any amount of streamlining or popularizing of museums as we know them would render them adequate for what the future may hold.

If what I am saying looks like an excuse for not trying to foretell the shape of things to come, consider how easily we may fall into error by too confidently outlining what we mean to do. We

169

hear much about the problem of leisure. Industrialists, sociologists, even governments declare we will have more and more time on our hands, that we must be educated to enjoy it, and it is being said museums will play an important part in this vast, time-killing exercise. Laudably in my view, the Schumacher school, believing personal satisfaction in work to be more important than mere production, regards the prospect of boundless leisure as disastrous. Work, Coomaraswamy has said, is to the higher faculties as food to the body. If this philosophy is as sound as increasing numbers in their hearts feel it to be, it is the nature of work which will have to undergo profound change for the sake of human contentment and happiness, and it is for a new sort of work-pattern that the race will have to be re-educated, not for leisure. This is going to be fundamental to any re-thinking of the function of museums, and the further we are led into directing them along what may prove the wrong road the further we will have to come back.

Speculation about museums and the school system likewise is called in question in its fundamentals because education itself is coming under searching new examination. To quote Schumacher, education would be 'the transmission of ideas of value, of what to do with our lives', the transmission of 'know-how' taking second place. Already I have said in Chapter V that I believe training in values in discrimination, is one of the present duties of museums. If it be accepted, then, that the broad remit of museums is to serve the community, we have to know more about the sort of community we are going to have.

If what I have written amounts in fact to advocacy of keeping the options open as long as possible, or preserving maximum flexibility and room for manoeuvre, are there ways in which we can usefully anticipate the problems awaiting us in this rather murky future?

In the first place, we must guard against the temptation to turn museums into something else. Much of what the foregoing chapters contain may seem to suggest that as long as museums can attract and inform large numbers of visitors, the collections can almost be allowed to recede into the background. Such an impression would be quite wrong. It is only because in this country our collections are taken so much for granted, to the neglect of their interpretation, that I have put special emphasis on this last. Things are quite different in the United States, where such a warning about turning museums into something else may well be necessary, and is in fact uttered by Duncan F. Cameron when he writes: 'One of the most visible trends in the "museum revolution" in North America has been the creation of non-museums, by which I mean exhibit and activity centres concerned with public education through the medium of the exhibit, but without dependence on collections of original materials.' In my time as a museum director I made a point of refusing all temporary exhibitions consisting wholly or mainly of two-dimensional exhibits: photographs and graphics, supplemented by audio-visual aids. There is a great number of those in circulation. I refused them because they were not the stuff of museums, although some who offered them obviously believed they were helping to offset museum 'stuffiness'! It is no part of my case in the first chapter that ideas should supplant collections, but that they should interpret the collections. Where museums have the advantage over other institutions concerned with education, and indeed over films however well produced, is that their stock-in-trade is the real things which make up creation itself. The museum must find its fulfilment *as* a museum.

Then we must be ready to tailor museums to the communities they have to serve. Established urban communities are natural environments for the larger museums, not only because with their research responsibilities such museums need the supporting institutions, but because they are focal points for great numbers of visitors from other countries; yet those urban communities contain large numbers of people of simple tastes and little education who could benefit from a different, smaller type of museum. And it must not be overlooked that perhaps twice as many people dwell outside those conurbations, so that the smaller museum must in future come into its own, otherwise forty millions are going to be without any museum service at all.

The majority of those people live in populous areas, few of which have museums worth the name. Many are new areas. The new towns of the United Kingdom total twenty-nine. Whether, like Stevenage or Crawley, they are linked to existing urban areas or whether, like Milton Keynes and Livingstone, they are intended to be new 'cities', they do not have, and cannot easily acquire, the sort of cultural backgrounds which great, old-established cities or which ancient, unspoilt rural communities possess. Without such backgrounds the quality of life is unsatisfactory, and they cannot be laid on like water and electricity. Culture, like prosperity, has to be fostered, not imported. And cultural aid schemes tend to be a little too like the economic aid given by the West to the Third World: too sophisticated for the ordinary man's use, and likely to improve the lot of the 'haves' rather than the 'have-nots'. Raymond O'Malley writing of the Highlands, long ago pointed the danger to an existing folk culture of importing arts which do not belong; and although a new town area has no folk culture to destroy, it is far better to generate something new which can live and belong there than to transplant cultural activities which have no relevance.

I hasten to say I am not criticizing the choirs and youth orchestras and the like which some of those towns have produced, to their great credit. But deep down there must be a real basis to seek for, roots to discover on to which to graft, local traditions, history, natural features to lay bare and learn about; and if the developers have obscured all this by imposing a concrete wilderness it is all the more important to get beneath it. Here is where the importance of the small museum could lie. In Chapter XVI I have made a plea for the expansion of the local museum to become a focus for the effort to discover identity. At first this will need much outside help and missionary zeal. In a new town one enterprise must support another, at least in the formative stages, and the museum could be part of a complex including theatre, lecture hall, adult education centre. But here too the museum must develop as a museum.

I assume the continuing development of some form of national museum service in this country as referred to in Chapter XVI. It may be worth while to repeat my reservations about a 'vertical' organization with priority given to the large museums, benefits eventually to be passed on to the small museums. It is in the administrative tradition to filter aid and advice down through a hierarchy with responsibilities which diminish tier by tier, and I have queried this and complained that many local museums cannot wait until such a system is fully organized and operating. I might add a *caveat* about the danger of regimentation. Perhaps what is needed is to revitalize the British tradition of leaving things to local initiative, but with a sharp watch kept to be sure it is exerted. It will have to be encouraged by prompting, and by money and advice at regional and at district levels, and only where it fails to materialize by stepping in and creating a growth-point.

The nation-wide vitality which impresses anyone visiting the museums of the United States stems from the national pattern of life. Washington may be the capital, New York the largest city, but from coast to coast, even in small places, there are spontaneous initiatives which owe nothing to distant centres. So far as public access to the finest museum material in any field of discipline is concerned, therefore, there is a very healthy distribution, not only of the material itself but of scholars working on it and inter-preting it. The cultural centralization which the United Kingdom suffers from is quite exceptional, and the consequent distinctions between metropolitan and provincial—now often rather ridicu-lously disguised as 'regional'—have created deprivations and imbalances which will certainly have to be corrected before any satisfactory replanning can be undertaken. The Shetlander and the Londoner are equal under the law, but in the things which are bought with their taxes they are not equal, among them access to an adequate museum service. I have already scouted the notion of a massive redistribution of existing collections, but there could be a redistribution of support for the smaller museums from central funds. Even in the United States the need for federal financial support is stressed by the Belmont Report (1969). Local authorities will have to be subsidized and made responsible for a museum service as they are for educational facilities and for health, security and other services. The national museum service would have the duty of co-ordinating, of inspecting conditions, of counselling, but certainly not, I trust, of imposing a rigid pattern on museums large and small.

It might be worth while dwelling briefly on what are coming to be thought of as the regional museums, at present the museums of the big provincial cities. I have indicated that in the United States the people of Massachusetts, California, Illinois, Kansas, even the Deep South, have reasonably easy access to museum material of the first class, and the same distribution is true of certain European countries, notably Germany and Italy, also Holland, despite her small size. Several of our city museums in this country have collections of international interest. If they are to receive encouragement from central funds, how are they to develop? In a country as small as ours there would seem to be little sense in fostering the same range of representation in eight or ten cities, with subsequent petty rivalries. In the technological sphere it is obvious each should emphasize the technology of its own regional industries. In the spheres of archaeology and art this may be possible, if to a more limited extent, but some of our municipal collections of foreign art are of considerable repute, and this could be a pointer. More than ten years ago in *The Guardian* Joseph Darracott advocated a policy of adding to existing strengths. He was dealing mainly with painting, but one thinks of how Bristol's already good oriental collection might be built up as Philadelphia's has been, of how in Glasgow the Burrell Collection's European tapestries and stained glass, already magnificent could be made a centre for the study of such things.

In the early chapters I have insisted that museums are not collections, neither are they buildings. With an eye to the future, my first priority would be people. It is Dr Wittlin's first priority also: 'Let us call a moratorium on the expansion of buildings and on the acquisition of additional gadgetry until we know more about the benefits people derive from what is going on in museums.' And of course people are the first priority of the Schumacher school in the world at large. Museums, like everything else in a sane world, must be for people. This is perhaps the only sure yardstick we have to measure what we do and propose to do in the midst of so much uncertainty. Indeed we should make a virtue of necessity in these inflationary times and throw the effort which might have been spent on planning costly new buildings or negotiating for expensive acquisitions into closer study of the real needs of the people in whose name most museums are now operated. However, I have reservations about assessing what people need in the American way. 'Is it not the social scientist to whom we must turn first for guidance?' asks Cameron. 'A psychologist specialising in visual perception is needed,' counsels Wittlin. As early as 1928 the American Association of Museums published *The Behavior of the Museum Visitor* based on three years of psychological studies. Here I can only revert to what I have advocated more than once: that a museum in some degree at least must be a work of art in its own right. Creativity should be evident in all its public galleries and its public activities, not only in their general scope but in every detail. This is the force which can and must bring it alive, and which will evoke response in those who pass through its doors.

Not all the psychologists and psychiatrists and social scientists in the registers, no matter how deeply they have studied human responses to this and that, can do anything to help generate the creative spark in the backrooms of our museums. Indeed they are more likely to inhibit the spark. An artist or a craftsman can work within the framework of a specific commission to fill that window or this niche or the panel in a ceiling, may even be stimulated by the challenge of it; but if he is to satisfy a psychiatrist that his work will elicit the right responses from the average viewer he will turn to another sort of job. The museum's requirements are restriction enough. They pose plenty of problems to discipline fancy and imagination. I am not trying to close the doors of the museum to any advice from such specialists, and there might well be room for them, for example, in studies of sensory perception in the field of the handicapped; but in general terms I believe the museum must still stand or fall by interpreting its material through the vision and skills of the men and women behind the scenes. If they have something to say, let them say it direct; if they have nothing to say they are in the wrong job. Chances of success are heavily loaded in favour of the museum by the very reality and richness of the possessions which it has to offer.

And here, of course, we come back to this factor, people. We must have the right people to do the interpreting, the right people to co-operate with them at every level. In this perhaps we can do something practical to insure the museum will be equipped to deal with future situations as they arise: to recruit and train the right people, and make sure they get their opportunities. This is not a counsel of perfection. Every museum generation throws up some of the right people, and their achievements—restricted too often, maybe, by circumstances—have been there for all to see. What we have to do is to decide who constitute the right people, then to make sure there are more and more of them. Their talents and skills apart, they should be the sort of people who assess work by what they can put into it rather than by what they get out of it. So far is the popular image of museums from the truth, those institutions can offer a way of life which makes the average profession or calling of today deadly dull by comparison, and that is some part of the reward.

175

Short Bibliography

T. R. Adam: *The Museum and Popular Culture.* New York, 1939

Germain Bazin: *The Museum Age.* Brussels, 1967

Michael Brawne: *The New Museum.* London, 1965

Germaine Cart, Molly Harrison, Charles Russell: *Museums and Young People.* Paris (ICOM), 1952

Laurence Vail Coleman: *Historic House Museums.* Washington, D.C., 1933

Laurence Vail Coleman: *The Museum in America.* 3 vols., Washington, D.C., 1939

John Cornforth: *Country Houses in Britain—Can they Survive?* London, 1974

A. Leveillé: *Scientific Museums.* Paris (ICOM), 1948

S. F. Markham: *Report on the Museums of the British Isles (other than national museums).* Edinburgh, 1938

Sir Henry Miers: *Report on the Museums of the British Isles (other than national museums).* Edinburgh, 1938

Muscums Association: *Museums and Art Galleries—a National Service.* London, 1945

A. E. Parr: *Mostly About Museums.* New York, 1959

Paymaster-General and Others: *Future Policy for Museums and Galleries.* London, 1971

Standing Commission on Museums and Art Galleries: *Survey of Provincial Museums and Galleries.* London, 1963

Standing Commission on Museums and Art Galleries: *Universities and Museums.* London, 1968

UNESCO: *The Organization of Museums—Practical Advice.* Paris, 1960

Ann White: *Visiting Museums.* London, 1968

Alma S. Wittlin: *Museums: In Search of a Usable Future.* Cambridge, Mass., and London, 1970

Alma S. Wittlin: *The Museum, its History and its Tasks in Education.* London, 1949

The Museums Journal, London; *Museum,* Paris; *Museum News,* U.S.A.

Index